GET A KLU

IN 52

A Practical Guide
to Expanding Self & Business

Jeffrey Klubeck

GETA KLU IN 52:
A Practical Guide to Expanding Self & Business
Jeffrey Klubeck

First Edition Copyright © 2019 by Jeffrey Klubeck

Second Edition Copyright © 2020 by Jeffrey Klubeck

ISBN: 978-1-7330862-2-6

Cover design by Sean O'Connor
OhSeeDesign@gmail.com

Editing, Typography, and Layout by Patti McKenna
Pattimck6@gmail.com

Printed in the United States of America

DEDICATION

I DEDICATE THIS BOOK to some amazing women, mentors, and friends…

…to Mary Ann, just showing up made me want to be a better person and THEN you decided to support me every step of the way … unreal…

…to Abigail, when you are ruling this world, please remember how hard Dad worked to set a good example … and thank you for the endless inspiration that you are…

… to Mom, I am so glad I published the first edition while you were with us…in this 2nd edition, I am equally dedicated to making you proud … rest peacefully with Dad, and thank you for everything…

…to Sue, the months preceding the 2nd Edition of this book are months I do not know how I would have gotten through without you … the most patient, loving, compassionate, diplomatic and "healer" of a listener I have ever known … it's you! …

…to Robyn, the revolution may not be televised, but the gatherings WILL be gifted … for sharing your gifts with me at a time I needed them most I'll be forever grateful…

…to Patty and Charlie, your commitment to being online with me EVERY WEEK in 2020 for the live readings of each tip is something that I will be forever grateful for … what a year we shared in such a unique way … thank you so much for showing up every week!

...to Maresa, thank you for all your help with the fist edition of the book ... "done" was certainly better than "perfect"... and I certainly would not have started or finished the first version without you. Thank you so much for continuing to believe in me as we take this thing to new heights...

...to Dr. Real, thanks for helping me see the best in myself (except for when you bagging on me in front of Mary Ann to keep me in check, of course) ... to have such a deep and loving relationship with "my professor" over all these decades is a priceless blessing in my life ... you mean the world to me...

...to Greg, thanks for inviting me into "big boy" conversations about authoring and the personal growth industry... I couldn't be more grateful and eternally wish you all the best...

...to Bennett, I'm not sure if you know that I consider you a mentor, and this might be a pretty cool way to find out ... from being a family man, a businessman, and most definitely a Lakers Fan, I owe you the world for all that has come of our friendship ... love you so much, brother...

...to Jim, you believed in me enough 20 years ago to mentor me as a Recruiter, and 15 years later, you believed in me enough to hire me to coach/train your entire company ... you represent an amazing professional journey for me and are an icon for friendship and values ... thank you...

... to Dave, it will be hard to ever really explain how much of my motivation comes from you ... from wanting to protect myself from you, to wanting to beat you, to wanting to make you proud, you have always been one of my biggest sources for "drive/determination" ... thanks, big bro!

...to Dr. T-Bone, ... oh, Doctor! What a huge burden it can be to mean SO MUCH to another human being ... thanks for willingly sharing that burden with me... #KluBone...

...to A.J., the first edition of this book came out at a time in your life where it seemed you were "getting it"... as you transitioned from middle to high school, we saw so many of the right habits, perspectives, and decisions from you … you are a sophomore as this second edition comes out and I couldn't be prouder of what you accomplished as a freshman! I know you are destined for your own versions of greatness … keep working hard, getting good grades, stay committed to making others better and your greatness is assured … I love you…

…to Brody, knock knock [who's there?] … zure [who's zure?] Who's Your Daddy?! A ha ha ha ha! I love telling knock knock jokes and playing games with you … maybe one day you will write a book, too. Always remember, when opportunity knocks, you always open that door … I love you…

…to Dad, your dedication to Mom and our family was a model of greatness that I truly cherished beyond words … thank you for trusting me to carry the Klubeck loyalty forward…I got it under control and won't let you down…thank you so much, Pops … I love you!

…to my students/clients—all of you past, present, and future—your growth is THE reason I do what I do … your success is THE reason … for all of it … so please be fearless in your continued commitment to personal and professional growth my friends … all my love…

Jeffrey

FOREWORD

JEFF KLUBECK AND I first crossed paths just before the turn of the millennium. At the time, I was an established headhunter working for an executive search firm in Carlsbad, California. Jeff was a wet-behind-the-ears newbie who was assigned to be my protégé. He was a great student and a natural sponge: He soaked up everything he could learn. Jeff's gregarious extroversion makes him a natural salesman. The only credit I can claim is having shared a little bit of my knowledge to fine-tune his sales techniques and build his organization skills.

We worked on some projects that demonstrated our independent qualities. In the world of contingency search, we learned and honed our pitch to close "container" searches—which is a hybrid of contingency and retained searches. In contingency search, a headhunter only gets paid to find a person that gets hired. With a retained search, you get paid regardless of whether the candidates are hired or not. We were the first in our company and one of only a handful of headhunters in our industry that offered this unique win-win solution. The hybrid approach got us paid up front. That allowed us to really dive deep in to a difficult, time-consuming search, while still giving the client company security of not paying two-thirds of the fee unless we successfully filled the position. I mention this because it's an early example of Jeff doing something different, out of the mainstream, and focused on offering a better client-focused solution unique from the rest of his industry.

Fast-forward 15 years …

Right after assuming my current position as Chief Operating Officer at Etching Expressions, Jeff and I reconnected. For me, this followed a string of starting several businesses, changing careers, relocating, and finally returning to San Diego. Jeff was in the early stages of his coaching career and still teaching at City College of San Diego. Kick-starting his marketing, Jeff was offering free sales seminars for real estate agents. Liking the topic, I invited Jeff to present the training for my sales staff, as the subject matter was spot on. We started with a few training sessions and then added more (and more). The foundation was being laid.

We started with identifying 1, 2, and 3s. We practiced developing an elevator pitch and building a toolbox of phrases and compelling benefits to present to customers. We DISC tested the entire sales staff so we could map out personalities. We learned what to expect out of each other based on our natural personality strengths and inclinations. Most important, we learned how to communicate with each other and customers much better.

Quickly, our ad hoc sessions turned into regularly scheduled trainings. As we delved into organization and better self- and team-management, my production supervisors joined in. Soon they had their own sessions with topics including SMAART goal setting, meeting agendas, people-centered communication ("please and thank you"), and the importance of job aids. Finally, we added an executive component where the top leadership had our own monthly coaching session focused on strategy and accountability. By this time, we had meetings scheduled every week for different departments. It all worked exceptionally well since Jeff had a complete 360° view of the entire company. What insight he could get from one department immediately transferred to another, such that Jeff really understood the inner workings of the company from all angles. This was invaluable in addressing challenging issues, giving examples, and understanding how all the personalities fit together.

Jeff's intensive trainings and coaching—sharing and getting us to apply the principles and tips in this book—resulted in immediate and long-lasting effects to our bottom line. In the first two years after engaging with Jeff, we experienced back-to-back sales growth rates of over 40% per year—more than doubling our sales. Importantly, our production staff got much better organized. This resulted in a string of four years of consistently better productivity. During that time, our labor hours *decreased* by 20%, while our production throughput *increased* by 15%. In other words, by getting 15% more work done with 20% less labor, productivity shot through the roof. All because people were better trained, managers were more organized, and communication among work-centers increased.

What I love about Jeff's method is that, while many of his nuggets of wisdom are not necessarily earth shattering, the perspective and way he presents the topic is unique, eye opening, and meaningful. Take, for example, the eminently simple concept of identifying prospects as a 1, 2, or 3.This is now so ingrained in our sales culture it effortlessly slips out when discussing prospects. Another great nugget is to know the drivers of buyer psychology. When presenting to a prospect, don't just focus on the features and benefits, but really speak to and address their emotional needs such as certainty, variety, connection, etc. This now guides our customer engagement strategy at every turn. Where previously, we loaded communication down with a ton of features, we realized we were not addressing, connecting with, and satisfying the emotional needs of the customer. The result is a more coherent and effective communication strategy.

I encourage you to read, sit with, and reflect on the tips Jeff presents in this book. To put the skills into action and really see a transformation in yourself or your organization. Do the work. If Jeff suggests to "Ask questions!," write down every possible answer that prospects want to know or need to know to make a decision. Then formulate appropriately wordsmithed questions and have them at the ready. Do this and your confidence will increase, your customers will notice, and your sales will bloom.

Jim Ristuccia, COO
Etching Expressions
San Diego, California

TABLE OF TIPS

NETWORKING

SALES

ACCOUNTABILITY

Dear Growth Seeker,

The mantra I held to when writing/publishing the first edition of this book was, "done is better than perfect." I lived with imperfections, "missings," and mistakes as embarrassing as misspelling my OWN name … but none of it overtook the pride I felt in getting it DONE! A favorite #KloobySnack of mine is that there is no such thing as a mistake, just "learning" wrapped in a little discomfort. So, I learned a lot in the process of self-publishing my first book.

None of that is to say that this, the second edition, is perfect. It is not. It is simply better. Better formatting … better ordering of the sections … better layout … better editing … better picture selection and placement …better cover design (that's subjective, but still better in MY opinion) …and better value as this edition contains a preview chapter of my next book: *The Integrity Game*!

The most awesome thing about the first edition of the book was the community I was able to build around it on Facebook. As I type this note, over 600 people joined the "Get A Klu in 52" group on Facebook, where I would stream a LIVE reading of one tip per week every week in 2020. Yeah, 2020 … every single Sunday in 2020, I got onto Zoom and livestreamed into the Facebook group … and in all 52 readings, I was joined on the Zoom side by some very loyal fans of my work, which made for dynamic group discussions around the content each week. It was a journey that I will be repeating in 2021 …except I will be streaming into my YouTube Channel ("watchgetaklu") this time, instead of Facebook. I hope you can join on Zoom or YouTube for those. I will continue to nurture and add value to the Facebook group for the book, and I hope you join, if you haven't already.

So, the mantra this time around is: The largest room in the world is the room for improvement! I hope you enjoy this second/improved version of *Get A Klu in 52*, and I hope you LOVE the teaser chapter for *The*

Integrity Game as much as I do. I have rarely been as excited about anything in my professional career as I am about producing *The Integrity Game* in all its forms … starting with the book. Dig it.

Finally, thank you so much for any time you are investing in this work … in yourself! There are TONS of places to go for personal/professional growth content, so the fact that you are here and believe there is value here for you means the world to me! Accept my deepest and sincerest wish that you enjoy the 2nd Edition of *Get A Klu in 52*! Thank you!

To your success,

Jeffrey Klubeck

COMMUNICATION

IT'S ONE THING TO SAY "GO THERE" BUT IT'S THE RIGHT THING TO SAY "GO THERE - HERE'S A MAP"

COACH JEFFREY KLUBECK

*Communication is the central
nervous system of all relationships!
Jeffrey Klubeck*

*The single biggest problem in
communication is the illusion that
it has taken place!
George Bernard Shaw*

T I P #1

CHECKING BAGGAGE!

We all bring baggage to communication.

Imagine three suitcases. One of them is labeled "Heredity," and it represents our physical characteristics that we were born with (piercings, tattoos, implants, nips, tucks, infusions, or other modifications notwithstanding.) These are the things we had no choice over (you can believe that I did not volunteer myself into the "balding" line at the heredity check-out!).

A second suitcase is labeled "Culture," and it represents—are you ready for this?, "The totality of learned and accumulated experience that is shared by a population and transmitted socially from generation to generation." Said another way, our values, attitudes, beliefs, and ways of doing and being. When it comes to culture, there is plenty that we are born into without our choice. As we get older, there are other aspects of culture that we adopt or choose to include in our lives.

The third suitcase is labeled "Personal/Past Experiences" and represents everything that has ever happened to us individually, including things we may not remember. Whether or not we have ever been bitten by a dog in the past will influence any communication or experience having to do with dogs in the present.

Of these three suitcases, only Heredity is immediately visible when we interact with others. If we can see, we know someone's skin color, height, body type, hair color, and so forth—and those factors influence the interaction. The rest—culture and personal history—must be discovered.

A lot of miscommunication occurs when people fail to be open to our curiosity about another's culture or background, when people assume that everyone either is or should be just like themselves. This failure to allow for the infinite possibilities of what others may have been or are currently going through in their lives gets in the way of effective communication.

Failure to celebrate or appreciate the merits of different ways of doing/being can lead to negative communication. The tip here is to understand that we all show up to communication with these three suitcases.

Understanding baggage categorically in terms of our heredity, culture, and history of personal experiences is one way to quickly understand another person. In *7 Habits of Highly Effective People*, Stephen Covey taught us to, "Seek first to understand, then to be understood." We ALL have baggage ... and we all bring it to communication!

T I P #2

INVITE ALL YOUR SENSES!

 Listening is a party, and I encourage you to invite ALL of your senses … not just hearing.

When I first started teaching communication classes in the late 1990's, the textbooks were telling us that listening was an active process that can be seen in stages. It started with hearing—when the sound is detected (sensed) by the eardrum. The next phase is attending—when you pay attention to what you are hearing so you may arrive at understanding — when you make meaning of what you have sensed/heard/attended to.

Because of how long-term memory works, immediately following our understanding of something is our remembering of it-when it gets stored in the vault of personal/past experience I referred to in Tip #1. This is a hyper-fast phase because it doesn't require our attention the way the previous phase understanding does or the following phase of "evaluating"—when we decide how we feel about what we have decided the meaning is of what we have heard, observed, and attended to. Following? Okay.

Ultimately, the last phase of listening is actually not listening at all; it is responding—when our reaction to what we have observed is the evidence of the meaning we have made and so forth. In short: hearing, attending, understanding, remembering, evaluating, and responding. There you have what I call the 6 "ings" of listening.

So, it is easy to talk about the distinction between hearing, which is the passive physiological process of sensing the sound waves, vs. listening, which is the active psychological process of understanding and responding to what we hear. It dawned on me a couple years in that if we replaced the word "hearing" with "observing," we could invite ALL of our senses to the Listening Party!

There is a joke or platitude that asks why God gave us two ears and one mouth … have you heard it? Yeah. Because we should spend twice as much time listening as we do talking. And I believe that wholeheartedly. What I dislike about the saying is that it tricks us into thinking that we listen with our ears—we don't. We HEAR with our ears, but we LISTEN with our mind!

Listening that involves all six phases (or even just the second phase, attending) is a mental/psychological process. Hearing is just a sense. We also attend to things we taste, touch, smell, and see. A deeper dive on the topic of listening would involve knowing the purposes of listening, the barriers to listening, the forms of non-listening, and tips for active-critical listening. I hope to interact with you in coaching or at one of my events to take you on that journey. For now, I want to invite you to invite all of your senses to the Listening Party in understanding the true difference between hearing and listening.

TIP #3

OVERCOME THESE,
AND YOU'LL OVERCOME A LOT!

 There are five tendencies we are all guilty of that suffocate objectivity, listening and, dare I say, loving! One of my college mentors, Dr. Larry Samovar, taught me the following five barriers to critical thinking which have a huge potential for "dark-side" communication (verbal aggression, name-calling, bigotry, and shaming, to name a few).

First is *Stereotyping*, which is when we have observed (or learned about) characteristics that may exist in one member of a population and then assuming that characteristic lives in all members of that population. The examples are usually, if not always, negative and categorical by race, gender, religion, sexual preference, and so forth. They are born in partial truth but are not 100% true across the entire population and can be funny at a stand-up comedian's show where the context is set for humor, but deep down they are dangerous due to how wrong/hurtful they can be.

A second personal tendency that prevents objective, loving, critical communication is being stubborn or what the literature would call *Frozen Evaluations*—when we have made up our minds about something and then are either too lazy or too proud to consider any information that might contradict the original opinion. At its worst, frozen evaluations can have people ignoring and discrediting the objective truth because it is too much work or pain to have to see the world any differently. Personally, I will watch FOX and CNN after a major political speech by a president, wanting to understand the talking points on all sides and with a curiosity if there is a way to see the speech differently than my original opinions. Most people get stuck in their ways and give credibility to sayings like, "Can't teach an old dog new tricks."

Are you guilty of being too stubborn? We all are. Can we reduce our stubbornness to be open and curious about other ways of seeing things? You bet. If what you believed to be true were not true, how soon would you want to know?

A third behavior is called *Self-Interest*, where we ignore or block out any information that doesn't appeal to our interests, which is failing to create new interests. How many times do you ask someone to try something you have discovered, and you see them resist right away, even when you KNOW they will love it? Think about how quickly you will change channels when channel surfing on TV—sometimes in less than a second or two. If it doesn't appeal to our immediate interests, we disconnect. I recommend always being open to being interested in new things and surrounding yourself with people who are, as well.

A fourth behavior that creates bad communication is called *Ego-Defense*, where we ignore or attack any communication that is not consistent with our current sense of self. Imagine the physical fight or flight response that makes us attack or run from physical danger and continue to imagine flinching when a bee buzzes by your ear or flinching and swatting at the same time to protect yourself, and then seeing it is a fly instead of a bee. Meaning, you weren't in any danger at all but instinctively protected yourself anyway.

My favorite example is walking into a spider web face first ... FREAKING OUT ... jumping around and wiping myself off frantically hoping there is no spider on me, sometimes even taking off my shirt and shaking it all around like folding bedsheets, then washing my hands and using the wet paper towel to wipe my face, head, and neck. Now totally certain that there is not spider on me, I walk underneath the air conditioning vent and felt my own hair get blown onto my ear and

IMMEDIATELY start jumping around and frantically slapping at my ear in case it was that damn spider … when all along it was my own hair.

Can you visualize that? The point is that we often attack or run from things that are not an actual threat to us physically just because we are hard-wired to protect ourselves, otherwise called the Survival Instinct. In communication we often attack or ignore people or ideas because instinctually we perceive them as a threat to our current state of being or sense of self. It's amazing how quickly we will call a person or idea dumb, stupid, lame, foolish, or any negative adjective before we'd ever stop to just ask: I wonder what is awesome about that different way of doing things than how I do it. I would bet money that the greatest amount of bad communication is produced by instinctual ego-defense vs. open, curious, vulnerable, and loving communication.

Finally, when groups of people are doing what individuals do during ego-defense it can be referred to as *ethno-centrism*. "Ethno" means culture and "centrism" is the placing of something in the central position of importance. So, ethnocentrism is essentially the dangerous and mistaken belief that one's culture is superior to all other cultures. It should go without saying how dangerous this belief/behavior can be. I am a big fan of being proud of your own culture, beliefs, politics, religion, or whatever. But when we believe those things about ourselves to be superior to differences in those things among others, it leads to things like fascism, racism, sexism, nationalism, and the cruel acts that a sense of "superiority" falsely justifies. The negative consequences of ethnocentrism at their worst lead to groups like the KKK or Hitler's Nazi culture.

Remember that we are all hard-wired to protect ourselves and that is how these tendencies are possible at all. Undetected and without conscious practice avoiding them we are vulnerable to making terrible mistakes in our communication. I strongly recommend learning more about these barriers to critical thinking, listening, objective, and loving communication!

T I P #4

REPLACE STATEMENTS WITH QUESTIONS!

Better yet, become a master at asking questions!

Did you know that a human brain, once hearing a question, will always attempt to answer it? That's powerful because it means that questions are among the most commanding in a category of communication techniques called attention getters. Simply put, when you have someone's attention, communication is easier.

Another benefit to asking questions is what a wonderful choice they are in replacing statements. A fair amount of bad communication occurs when people make assumptions about things. Asking questions to show curiosity, humility, or even ignorance is sometimes more productive than erroneously forwarding an incorrect or offensive assumption.

Said another way, statements are about what I think, but a question is about what others think. It is absolutely critical in communication that you are more interested in what others have to say than what you have to say yourself. Let others be interested in what you have to say, but I propose that it is in our best interest to be MORE interested in what others have to say. Again, it is THEIR job to be interested in what we have to say.

If you read my tips on networking, you're aware of the questions I have already prepared that I know I am going to ask people at networking events—knowing that after the fourth or fifth question my interest in them has gotten them interested in me—and then they start asking about me. It gets better, because now I know which things about myself to share because I have already learned so much about the other person. So, instead of sharing something about myself hoping they are interested, I can share what I am fairly certain they will engage with because I have taken the time to get to know them first by asking questions.

We already know that listening is the most important of all the communication skills, so being great at asking questions means you'll have more to listen to! Again, what you choose to say and share with others will be calibrated and guided with what you have already learned about them. You'll seem more on-point, efficient, or somehow, intelligent as a communicator.

In my coaching practice, there is no greater tool at my disposal, nothing more responsible for my success with my clients, than my ability to ask great questions. Questions that clarify. Questions that probe. Questions that mirror. Questions that intervene. Questions that cheerlead. Questions that condition. Questions that confront. Questions that guide. Questions that question! And so on.

If you have experienced coaching with me or perhaps seen me speak (because I am always questioning my audience,) you know the power my questions have to focus your attention on the truth … the strategy… the action required … the reporting … the reasons … the barriers … the willpower … the discipline … the purpose … the goals … the milestone … the peer group … the results!

In Tip #6, we will talk about eye contact being the most powerful form of non-verbal communication … and I'll end this tip suggesting that questions are the most powerful form of verbal communication!

TIP #5

CSI COMMUNICATION!

Indulge me here as I set this up…

Have you ever seen those CSI shows? There used to be only one, it was called CSI (for Crime Scene Investigation). It was good. So, of course, they made a spin-off for another city … CSI Miami, I think … then CSI Los Angeles, I believe. The original was in CSI Las Vegas. When I would teach this "tip" in my classrooms I used to joke that I was sick of those shows because they weren't as good as the original and I wasn't going to watch again until they came up with CSI Tijuana!

I digress … back to my set up: The hook for the show was evidence! The "forensic evidence" gathered at crime scenes and the science/technology of crime solving interwoven into classic mystery plots. Who knew? The main attraction of a TV show wasn't the characters (the lead character for CSI Miami was unwatchable in my opinion) or the plots (recycled crime-drama stuff), but the EVIDENCE…" how a crime is solved or the truth becomes evident" from the supporting materials gathered at the scene WAS the star of the show.

So, Tip #5 (thank you, by the way, for indulging me) is to watch (or practice): CSI Communication! Pay attention to evidence and understand the role of supporting material in effective communication.

Imagine that for every statement you ever make there is someone there to immediately ask, "What makes you so sure?" Some claims by themselves are believable upfront, while others require supporting material sometimes referred to as evidence or proof. So, when writing, speaking in public, or even during interpersonal conversation, and DEFINITELY during any form of argumentation, it is really ideal to know forms of evidence and how to select and present back up for the claims you are making.

The common forms of evidence I teach speakers to use in their presentations include facts, examples (stories/anecdotes), analogies, statistics, testimonials, comparisons, and demonstrations.

Each of these forms of supporting material can strengthen the acceptability or believability of any claims you are making. When seeking to inform, persuade, influence, convince, motivate, or in some other way having what you are communicating accepted, I recommend thinking about and making good selections as to the evidence (no, not forensic evidence like blood samples or fingernail follicle, but the supporting material that makes arguments stronger) you'll be ready to provide!

TIP #6

EYE CONTACT IS POWER!

 What an argument for the most powerful form of non-verbal communication!

Next to touch (which occurs in intimate space), eye contact is the most effective way to show someone they have your attention. Paying attention to people—being concerned about and interested in others—is one of the greatest paths to leadership and influence ... being liked and trusted ... because you care, pay attention and SHOW that with sustained eye-contact and active listening!

Listening weaves its way into most of my communication tips, but this one is focused on that eye-contact ... the windows to the soul ... their magnetism ... their truth-telling clues ... their mystery and so on.

On a personal note, I have never looked more deeply into another person's eyes than when my wife went through her first of three C-sections with our first son A.J. The umbilical cord was wrapped around his neck, so he wasn't coming out after hours and hours of labor. We were scared. The doctor told us we'd have to do an emergency C-section. In the operating room, I sat on a little roller stool next to Mary Ann's head, as she lay flat on the operating table. On the other side of the vertically erected sheet at her torso was the cut they were making into her stomach to go in to pull out our child. Mary Ann and I were both so scared that all we did was look into each other's eyes the entire time from as close as our faces could possibly be while still being able to keep each other in focus…and she asked me to sing our favorite songs to her…but no matter what, do not break eye contact.

I hope my story gave you a sense of how powerfully connected two human beings are when making accurate, deep, and sustained eye-contact with each other. I am positive you already know that eye contact is powerful and have your own experiences of that power. The tip here is not to just know its power, but to practice making better eye contact … more often … deeper … more sustained … to practice and work at more eye contact in your conversations!

T I P #7

JOE LOVES MARY?

 Joe Loves Mary! Joe loves Mary? Joe? ... loves Mary?! JOE loves MARY!!! Joe ... loves ... Mary. Shhh ... joe loves mary shhh.

It's the same three words every time (assuming "shhh" and punctuation do not count as words), but I can say those same three words in a way that changes the meaning every time. Again, the words never change. You can do it, too. Ready to have fun? Go ahead.

Meaning #1: How would you say it if you were a kid teasing another kid (Joe or Mary) on an elementary school playground? That's right ... in that neener neener neener voice and rhythm. Okay.

Meaning #2: How would you say it if you were one of Mary's best friends and knew Joe was the man of her dreams? Yeah, with that rising inflection that is kind of celebratory ... kind of cheerful. Yep, okay

Meaning #3: How would you say it if you thought Joe was already dating Susan? Yeah, you'd put that vocal question mark at the end of it ... also a rising inflection, but in curiosity ... unlike the celebratory rising inflection of a bridesmaid SO happy for her bestie! You get the idea? The three words never change: Joe Loves Mary. But when we change our NON-verbal communication (everything OTHER than the words), we change the entire meaning!

The point here is that **(KloobySnack):** How you are saying what you are saying is, in fact, what you are REALLY saying! The meaning is not conveyed by the words, they are just the Trojan Horse (if you will) to usher in the non-verbal communication that gives us the REAL meaning! Letters are to be found in words, but meaning can be found in the non-verbal communication (including punctuation if text-only) with which those words are delivered.

Subtle changes to our pitch, tone, volume, projection, and range of steadiness to fluctuations in any given aspect will change the meaning of the expression. The same goes with posture, special body movement as well as gestures, facial expressions, and eye contact (or lack-thereof.) ALL have a huge impact on the meaning of our words.

Sometimes, our non-verbal will serve as repetition for the words we offer. Other times, it will contradict the words (such as sarcasm or irony.) A simple raise of the eyebrow acts to compliment or accentuate the words. Other times, non-verbal signals function to substitute for words, and they even help us protect ourselves and control our environments by use of space, positioning, gestures, and eye-contact (or lack thereof ... like when you walk by someone and avoid eye contact so you don't "have to" say hello).

It's a GREAT idea to read at least one book on non-verbal communication in this lifetime. I recommend anything by Dr. Peter Andersen (my former professor, great friend, and mentor) who has forgotten more about non-verbal communication than I have ever learned (and I taught the subject for 20 years!) And always remember that HOW you say WHAT you are saying is, in fact, what you are REALLY saying!

TIP #8

YOU'RE LISTENING TO W-I-I-F-M!

 Perhaps you've heard that saying before? Everyone's favorite radio station is WIIFM ... which stands for What's In It For Me!?

Or, if you prefer literature to radio, everyone is walking around this world ... Okay, not EVERYone ... but most people (and even if not most people, enough people!) are walking around this world auto-biographically, meaning the story in their head is THEIR story. So, instead of joking when mimicking a DJ on the radio saying, "You're listening to WIIFM," I am serious when saying, you are TALKING to WIIFM!

If whatever you are saying does not benefit the person you are talking to, you have lost a HUGE percentage chance that they will pay attention, or continue to pay attention, if the conversation does not benefit them or allow for their participation/input/perspectives/contribution.

Thankfully, for you talkers out there, there are people that LOVE to listen ... to be there for you ... that do not need to control a conversation or ever have it be about themselves. There is balance in the world when opposites come together like that. The rest of the time, it takes some mature communication skills to censor one's comments to only those that are selfless, inclusive, curious, inviting, complimentary, open/growth-minded, information-seeking, fun-loving, playful, and so forth.

Without paying attention to the role self-interest plays in communication, you may be speaking to deaf ears or actually possess the deaf ears or both. Yet people remain in one-way relationships or are constantly butting heads with others or sucked into other people's drama or any number of communication bummers that all stem back to the notion of self-interest: either failing to keep your comments in the realm of what others might be interested in OR failing to create an interest in what someone else is interested in—or combinations thereof.

If you can check yourself when you find yourself losing interest if the conversation isn't about you, or if you can make sure that when you speak it's in ways that interest, compliment, and invite others, you are going to be "that person" that others really want to be around.

Most people are just tuned in to WIIFM or walking around auto-biographically. Don't be like most people—be someone who is LIKED by most people—and you do that by being interested in THEM! Pick up *7 Habits of Highly Effective People* (Covey) or *How to Win Friends and Influence People* (Carnegie) for some classic reading on the role of "self vs. other interest" in effective communication!

T I P #9

GET EMOTIONAL!

In his "Modes of Persuasion," Aristotle created what we know as logos—the argument supported by reasoning and evidence; ethos—the credibility with which we make the argument; and the subject of this tip, pathos—the appeals a speaker makes to the emotions of their audience. Aristotle called it pathos—my communication professors called it "emotional appeals," and sometimes I have fun referring to it as "going psycho/emo."

The tip here is that the more you know about emotions, the better a communicator you will be. When I got answers to the following questions about emotions, my communication skills and ability to positively connect with and influence others skyrocketed, which, in turn, took my coaching practice from local to global ... from pretty good to world class.

Here are some questions about emotions that I recommend you get/know the answers to:

- Did you know that emotions are called feelings because we can literally/physically FEEL them?

- Do you know why different emotions feel differently (like anger feeling different than sadness even though both are negative, or satisfied feeling different than enthusiastic even though both are positive)?

- Do you know that, very simply put, emotions are chemicals?

- Do you know that there is a unique chemical combination for the major emotions we experience … a unique recipe, if you will, of chemical ingredients for emotions like jealousy, guilt, inadequacy, regret, shame, worry, frustration … as well as positive emotions, like joyful, hopeful, gratified, elated, pleased, adored, etc.?

- Do you know what part of the brain manufactures the chemicals associated with emotion?

- Do you know what triggers the hypothalamus into creating emotions?

- Do you know what happens when enough emotions are created in the hypothalamus to overflow?

- Did you know an emotion can dock-on (attach/insert itself into) cells in our bodies like a key in a lock or a syringe in a vein?

- Can you imagine how the chemicals of an emotion are injected into the nucleus of a cell it is docked-on?

- Can you begin to realize that (like alcohol or nicotine or sugar or cocaine or aspartame or any chemical from outside our body that we put in,) we can become addicted to the emotions we experience if we experience them often enough?

- Can you imagine that most of us, perhaps all of us, are addicted to one or more emotions?

- Are you familiar with Abraham Maslow's Hierarchy of Needs?

- Are you familiar with Tony Robbins' model of 6 Emotional Survival Needs (certainty, variety, connection, significance, growth, and contribution)?

As there is so much to learn about emotions, I could go on, but for this context my intent is not to ask or answer every question. Instead, I wanted to declare how important knowledge of emotions can be as a "top 10 tip" and to motivate your own interest in learning more about the role of emotions in communication.

Perhaps in my classrooms or at my events you have heard me share answers to these questions more fully … even better if we have applied the answers directly to your life/challenges/opportunities in 1:1 or group coaching. If not, I hope you make plans to explore the topic of emotions more fully and I hope to see you in one of the aforementioned contexts.

For now/this publication, be clear that the more you know about emotions—where they come from, what they are made of, how they differ from each other, how they vibrate and influence our biochemistry, how they influence meaning making and even our human magnetism to other people and events—the more likely you are to be an emotionally-intelligent communicator.

T I P #10

TELL THE TRUTH!

It's hard … but how hard is it?

Okay, it's really hard. We have so many influences in our life that promote "harmless" lying that we become desensitized to how often we lie … how comfortable we have become saying whatever comes to mind if it sounds good in our heads … whether or not it is true or based in any reality. There are hundreds of famous quotes about truth for good reasons. Here are some of my favorites:

- *The truth will set you free* (unknown).

- *Honesty is the first chapter in the book of Wisdom* (Thomas Jefferson).

- *Whoever is careless with the truth in small matters, cannot be trusted with important matters* (Albert Einstein).

- *It's better to be slapped with the truth than kissed with a lie* (Unknown).

- *Denying the truth doesn't change the facts!* (Unknown).

- *If you always tell the truth, you never have to remember anything* (Mark Twain).

- *If you never tell a lie, then you never have to play dumb* (Anthony Kiedis, Red Hot Chili Peppers).

- *Three things cannot be hidden: The Sun, The Moon and The Truth!* (Buddha).

- *You cannot hide your broccoli in a glass of milk* (a 5 year old).

As fun as it is to search for "truth quotes" online to select and include here, you get the idea now. We lie to avoid the consequences of our behaviors. We lie to influence others to our point of view or interests. We lie to live a different reality than reality. Some of us lie pathologically from mental illness, but most of us lie out of cowardice, fear, inadequacy, or some negative emotion that really makes healthy communication difficult. I believe it is only action/behavioral change that can truly (pun intended) change our circumstances for the better.

Making things up in our head and putting them out there as truth can be costly on so many levels. It is a waste of time for one. A simple dedication to reality allows you to change and improve circumstances quicker than the time it takes pretending things are fine/great.

Second, like Buddha says, truth (like the sun and moon) cannot be hidden. That is why sayings emerge like, "It will all come out in the wash" or "the truth will be revealed" or "all will be revealed." When the truth is revealed to contradict any lies you have told, you can no longer be trusted. There is nothing more important in a relationship than trust, and, therefore, perhaps nothing is more important when communicating than to always tell the truth!

NOTES

MARKETING

*It all comes down to finding potential buyers
and informing them ... find them,
inform them ... everything else is detail!*
Jeffrey Klubeck

*Stopping advertising to save money is like
stopping your watch to save time!*
Henry Ford

T I P #1

KNOW WHAT YOU NEED TO KNOW ...
THEN KNOW IT!

 There is a lot to know when it comes to marketing. So, my first marketing tip is to know what you are going to need to know and make a plan to know it!

Some of you might already know your customer really well, but you don't know exactly what you can promise that customer. Others of you know who your competition is and what they do well but haven't yet figured out how you are better or unique compared to them. Some of you know the locations your prospects will be but are unaware of the proper channels to reach them. Some of you know the features of what you are selling but struggle to explain the benefits. In either case, here is a short list of things I believe all marketers need to know:

- The 80/20 rule: 80% of value comes from 20% of parts ... meaning, there are 2 things on the list below that are more important to you than all the rest combined...

- Know your customers ... thoroughly!

- Know your competition ... so you can be better and different!

- Know the conditions ... what market conditions help/hurt your efforts?

- Know the issues your customers face!

- Know your products and services inside out!

- Know your brand ... your promise to the marketplace!

- Know the drivers of buyer (human) psychology!

- Know a wordsmith ... to avoid "death by jargon!"

- Know the difference between a brand and brandING!

- Know the channels ... along which to send marketing messages.

- Know location, location, and location ... to place your marketing messages where your prospects will be!

The list above is partial compared to everything a great marketer needs to know, but thorough and effective for anyone looking to improve as a marketer. Start with the 80/20 rule and look for the 2 items on this list you must make a plan to learn more about to get better right away!

T I P #2

KNOW YOUR (IDEAL) CUSTOMER(S)!

 There may be nothing more important to success in marketing than knowing your customer.

Demographics are your customer's observable traits (age, gender, socio-economic status, ethnicity, etc.). *Psychographics* refer to your customers' thought patterns, values, beliefs, and attitudes. It's also important to know behavioral patterns of customers, such as where they go and hang out and what else they shop for that may be related to your products or services.

The best marketers go further than that by creating buyer personas and customer avatars so as to get inside the mind of the customer — to truly understand their pain relieving or pleasure-seeking needs, their self-talk, their influencers, and so on.

Think of the hunter that is trying to "be the animal" so as to get a half step in front of the animal making that person the best possible hunter. Know your customer and you will know what to say, how to say it, where to say it and more! Everything in marketing starts with knowing your customer.

TIP #3

KNOW YOUR COMPETITION!

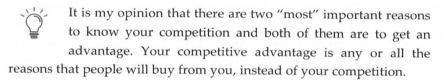 It is my opinion that there are two "most" important reasons to know your competition and both of them are to get an advantage. Your competitive advantage is any or all the reasons that people will buy from you, instead of your competition.

Broken down by these two reasons, ALL advantages are either what you do BETTER than your competition or what you do DIFFERENT than your competition. Of all the things that both you and your competition do/have/offer, what do you do, have, or offer that is BETTER than the competition? Or what do you do, have, or offer that your competition simply does NOT? Better or different!

Knowing your competition as intimately as possible will place you in the best position to create and maintain competitive advantages. This allows you to promote those advantages within your marketing messages. When you know your customer (Tip #2) and your competition, creating great marketing messages should be much easier.

Making sure you answer the following two questions in your marketing messages will keep your marketing on the right track: What problem do I solve and how do I solve it better/differently than anyone else?

T I P #4

KNOW THE CONDITIONS!

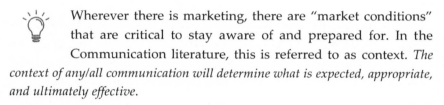 Wherever there is marketing, there are "market conditions" that are critical to stay aware of and prepared for. In the Communication literature, this is referred to as context. *The context of any/all communication will determine what is expected, appropriate, and ultimately effective.*

Knowing the context where marketing will take place serves the same purpose as helping marketers know what will be expected, appropriate and ultimately effective. Keep in mind that marketers are often most effective by creatively doing what is *NOT expected* or what is considered by some to be *inappropriate*!

These calculated decisions are always made with an awareness of external factors in the market. Asking or imagining how external forces such as the politics, economics, technology, international affairs, environment, or education will affect the mindset of prospects can be a difference maker in your marketing.

I believe great marketers will have their finger on the pulse of these external factors to understand how best to deliver the marketing message "given the context."

I encourage you to take time to #describethemarket ... to use real words to describe the market conditions that currently exist. Describe as much as you can about where your prospect is to be marketed to you (market conditions, physical surroundings, the situation, etc.), and you will have much more to work with when creating new and memorable ways to deliver your message.

T I P #5

KNOW THE ISSUES!

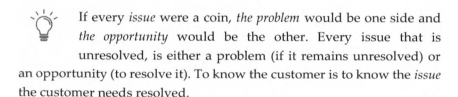 If every *issue* were a coin, *the problem* would be one side and *the opportunity* would be the other. Every issue that is unresolved, is either a problem (if it remains unresolved) or an opportunity (to resolve it). To know the customer is to know the *issue* the customer needs resolved.

However, there is an important difference between being considered an expert on your customer and being considered an expert on the *issue* your customers face. For example, knowing an entrepreneur needs to invest in work-life balance is not the same thing as knowing if the entrepreneur is married or single, in their 30's or 40's, a parent or with zero dependents, etc. Knowing entrepreneurs is different than knowing work-life balance.

The tip here is that the best marketers are not just great marketers ... they are also SME's (subject matter experts) regarding the issue customers might resolve with their products and services. A good marketer will know that the same type of person that is in the market for training bras might also be likely to buy concert tickets for a pop star or download certain social media app, but a GREAT marketer knows that same person is dealing with coming of age, identity, or peer group associations/pressure. A REALLY great marketer strives to know about those issues as much as the experts do!

T I P #6

KNOW YOUR STUFF!

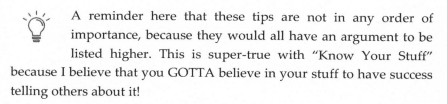A reminder here that these tips are not in any order of importance, because they would all have an argument to be listed higher. This is super-true with "Know Your Stuff" because I believe that you GOTTA believe in your stuff to have success telling others about it!

There's more to knowing your stuff than just believing, but it still starts there. Imagine knowing for a FACT that everyone that does not buy your products and services is worse off than those that do buy. Imagine knowing for a fact that your products and services do EVERYTHING you say they do ... and more! Imagine knowing for a fact that everyone who buys from you will believe they got WAY more value than what they paid or invested in.

When you have that knowledge that you are selling something amazing, your excitement, creativity, and commitment to telling the world about it is supercharged! So, one aspect of this tip is to BELIEVE in your stuff ... to know that it will work and be valued by your customer above its cost or investment.

The other aspect of this tip is to know the inner workings, details, and features of what you are selling.

As we have covered in other tips, it is one thing to know the customer, another thing to know the competition, another to know the market conditions, and still another to know the issues your customer is facing.

It is yet another thing entirely to have intimate knowledge of the product or service you are selling.

Ideally, you know exactly what the customer will get/experience/feel when interacting with your products and services. When you know your stuff that well, you are bound to have more options on how to effectively communicate to your prospects!

T I P #7

KNOW YOUR BRAND(S)!

 One of my mentors, Brian Tracy, taught me that: *your Brand is your promise to the marketplace*! So, another way of saying tip #6 is to, "Know your promises!"

Tip #6 asks you to focus on the *benefits* of what you are selling. People confuse features (tip #5) from benefits so allow me these examples: a feature of my coaching is accountability, but a benefit of my coaching is increased productivity. A feature of my strategic staffing consulting is candidate screening, but a benefit of my strategic staffing consulting is reduction in turnover and cost-per-hire.

The key question is what is the promise being made to the prospect? I coach my clients to infuse promises with the two qualities of being attention-gaining and sensational.

By attention-gaining, I mean speaking directly to the pleasure/pain relief desired by your prospect. *"Really*? You *could??"* is what you'd want a prospect to say after an attention-gaining promise.

By sensational, I mean the largest promise—the greatest promise—that you know you can back up! Because this is a marketing tip, don't get caught up in legal semantics of the word "promise"—it's used to provoke marketing messages, not legal and binding agreements.

So, what pain is your prospect in that you can relieve? What pleasure does your prospect seek that you can promise because of your company, team, stuff, self? Did you catch that at the end of the last sentence? Yeah, you can brand just about anything that creates a benefit for your customer. Meaning, I can brand myself (Coach Jeffrey) as having promises … I can brand my coaching or consulting or training as having promises … I can brand my team if I build or am on a team. Make sense?

Think about the IBM salesperson who promises to be the most responsive and ethical salesperson. The person who proudly announces his place on the most highly rated, experienced and professional technical field sales team that only IBM can assemble (branding the team) The one who is selling the most advanced, modern, efficient, cost and time saving machines on the planet (branding the product,) and who finally reminds you that it's ALL backed by IBM, the single largest machine company on the planet…so if anything goes wrong, you will have a replacement machine installed at your location before you can even finish calling in the problem (branding the company).

In future tips we go deeper on what promises are worth making and how to make them, but for now, understand that a brand is an attention-gaining, sensational promise that can be backed up that is made to the marketplace—and that your company, team, products/services, and self can ALL be branded! Great marketers will understand and keep all messages "on brand."

T I P #8

KNOW THE DRIVERS OF
BUYER (HUMAN) PSYCHOLOGY!

 Or, more simply put, a great marketer knows why people do what they do! It's fancy to say, "The drivers of our inner psychology" and much simpler to say, "What we all want!"

One of the reasons I love marketers so much is because, to be great, they MUST study the same basics of human motivation that we study and teach in the personal/professional growth industry. From our knowledge of behavioral style that can be measured with tools like DISC or Myers-Briggs, we know that marketing to Dr. Spock takes different messaging than marketing the same product and service to Jimmy Fallon.

Broadly speaking, people are either drivers, persuaders, promoters, supporters, coordinators, or analyzers. More broadly speaking, people are motivated by perfection, usefulness, freedom, control, service, tradition, or discovery (contact me to learn more about getting your own behavioral assessments conducted).

From our studies ranging from Aristotle, Maslow, Brian Tracy, or Tony Robbins, we know that psychological pleasure and pain is determined by the fulfillment of certain emotional needs. We know that people need certainty/safety, variety/excitement, connection/love, significance/power, growth/evolution, and contribution/legacy.

We also know that people form beliefs that determine their behaviors. We know that people can become addicted to the emotions they experience on a daily basis, and that is to say nothing of the chemicals outside of our bodies that we can become addicted to putting in.

This Tip, #8, is focused on the "inside job" of marketing … and to craft messages that truly speak to the prospects listening is to be an expert at the game of marketing! **(#KloobySnack)** To be a student of behavior is to be an expert in marketing!

T I P #9

KNOW A GOOD WORDSMITH!

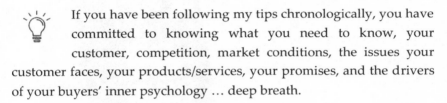 If you have been following my tips chronologically, you have committed to knowing what you need to know, your customer, competition, market conditions, the issues your customer faces, your products/services, your promises, and the drivers of your buyers' inner psychology … deep breath.

So, by now, you have learned a lot of jargon about each of those topics or categories. Jargon is the term that describes industry/subject-specific language—the language that students of the subject (or members of a culture) may understand readily, but non-students (members) would not.

Danger! Danger! Danger! You could be cursed! The curse of knowledge is when you are SO familiar with what you know that you have forgotten what it is like NOT to know what you know. That curse is a danger to great marketing! If marketing messages are full of jargon (words that only experts know the true meaning of), they risk NOT being understood and squander the opportunity to be memorable and lasting.

Allow me to exemplify: Nike isn't telling you to choose a shoe whose microfiber, mathematically-engineered, and spectrometer-calibrated, precision fit will have you wanting to overcome the inertia effect of human laziness and the undesirability of those among the species less physically fit than others. They are telling you to "Just Do It."

Do I need to provide another example? Okay. I do not promise that my coaching will (deep inhale) detect your diction choices to access your limiting beliefs, which I will then replace with empowering alternatives and condition (session by session) to the point of true and lasting (dare I say) trans-contextual transformation! No, but I WILL say, "Let's do a check-up from your neck up to get you out of your own way, off your ass and into action!"

So, like I said, you need a wordsmith and even better if you have a sloganeer on your side—someone who can string great words into memorable phrases that deliver your brand promise! Track these...

> #When it absolutely positively has to be there overnight!
> #The nighttime sniffling sneezing coughing aching nighttime fever so you can rest medicine!
> #I'm loving it!
> #Just Do It!
> #Where's the Beef?
> #Membership has its privileges!
> #Get A Klu!
> #Happy KLU Year!
> #KLUbrication makes things easier!

#With the right coach, you can have KLUcidity life and business!

#Some coaches go for the jugular, but Coach Jeffrey goes for the HUGular! #Know when to say WHEN!

I could go on, and clearly digress ...thanks for humoring me, let's turn to Tip 10.

T I P #10

MIND THE GAP:

BRAND VS. BRANDING!

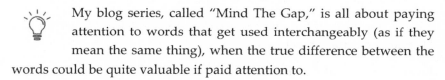 My blog series, called "Mind The Gap," is all about paying attention to words that get used interchangeably (as if they mean the same thing), when the true difference between the words could be quite valuable if paid attention to.

So, in a crossover tip, here I ask you to #MindTheGap between "brand" and "branding." Aside from the obvious that one is a noun and the other a verb, be clear that a brand is "the message" (your promise to the marketplace, remember?), whereas brandING is the totality of action aimed at putting brand messages into the marketplace.

If only for the time you will save in your meetings and dialogue with others about marketing, make sure you are all on the same page with your terminology. The brand is the promise. The branding is how the promise is sent/received in the marketplace.

When you are asking, "What is our brand?" You are not asking, "What is our branding?" I beg you to understand how much time you will save simply in knowing that distinction and making sure you share meaning around those terms with everyone on your marketing team.

Further benefits from this tip include a healthy division of labor between your techies (who want to know the technology to get the message out there) and the people-people more likely to be your wordsmiths and sloganeers (see tip #8).

Another reason to #mindthegap between brand and branding is so that each gets its fair and undiluted share of attention. When you are asking your brain for the words to communicate a promise, it will produce different answers than if you asked it for the best channels to deliver that message.

Branding sample from Etching Expressions

T I P #11

KNOW (OR CREATE) THE CHANNELS

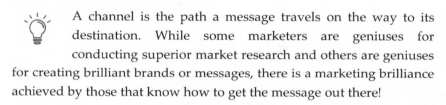 A channel is the path a message travels on the way to its destination. While some marketers are geniuses for conducting superior market research and others are geniuses for creating brilliant brands or messages, there is a marketing brilliance achieved by those that know how to get the message out there!

It was Marshall McCluhen who first told us, "The medium is the message," and this is a huge concept for marketers to grasp. My favorite exercise to exemplify this point is to imagine attending a major sporting event like a football game where there are over 50,000 people all in one spot for 3 - 4 hours and brainstorm a list of channels that exist in that one location.

I'll get you started: ad on the ticket stub, ads in the parking lot, ads on the give-away item that "all fans in attendance" receive ... how else? How else do marketers send a message to fans attending a sporting event? There are so many channels to get a message to a destination and marketers have gotten more and more genius about what counts as a delivery channel for marketing messages.

From the dividers that separate one person's groceries from another's in the checkout line in the supermarket to the TV's that now hover over the gas filling stations to SMS text messages on our smartphones, genius marketers will either choose or create the best paths along which to send their messages.

T I P #12

KNOW THE DESTINATIONS

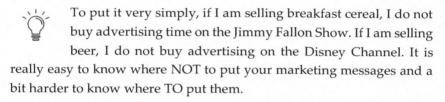 To put it very simply, if I am selling breakfast cereal, I do not buy advertising time on the Jimmy Fallon Show. If I am selling beer, I do not buy advertising on the Disney Channel. It is really easy to know where NOT to put your marketing messages and a bit harder to know where TO put them.

Very closely related to Tip #2 (Know Your Ideal Customer) is to know where they go ... where WILL they go ... where do they want to go ... where ARE they ... what do they pass enroute to where they are going? These questions will reveal more and more possibilities for where to put marketing messages, which, in turn, will give you even more choices on what channels you'll use to get the messages to those destinations.

In Tip #11, the pro sporting event exercise focused on all the channels that could be used or created to get a message to the fans attending the game. Well, it's intimate knowledge of the destination—the physical stadium itself as well as and what takes place there—that allows so much creativity for choosing and creating channels for marketing messages.

A marketer that knows exactly where the target customer will be and exactly what takes place AT the "where" is a marketer more likely to imagine or create the best messages and channels for that particular location, event, or experience.

Jack-in-the-Box has a promotion at Lakers' basketball games that if the Lakers win and hold their opponent under 100 points, all fans in attendance will receive a coupon for 2 free tacos when exiting the arena. The promotion is genius because the fans are reminded over the loudspeaker several times during the game. The message may flash on the scoreboard during timeouts and as the game nears completion, the crowd is chanting "TACO, TACO, TACO," urging the Lakers to play greater defense to keep the opponent under 100 points … and if successful, everyone leaves with physical vouchers with the Jack-in-the-Box branding all over it for the tacos that might stay in someone's car for days or weeks before its redeemed or thrown away.

It takes more than just knowing taco-eaters go to basketball games to come up with a promotion like that. Again, knowing where they will be and what happens at the where they will be is critical to genius marketing!

NOTES

NETWORKING

HOW TO FIND LEADS EVERYWHERE FOR YOUR
COACHING SERVICE

*Networking just doesn't work
without doing the
WORK of Networking!
Jeffrey Klubeck*

TIP #1

DEVELOP AN "ELEVATOR PITCH!"

 Or, as I prefer to say, "Know how you will be answering the #1 networking question: **What do you do?**"

It's more than just memorizing an elevator pitch. I coach people to master the *ingredients* of an elevator pitch more than any *single* pitch, which provides them dozens of ways to communicate their message conversationally without coming off robotic or pre-rehearsed.

The basic questions you should answer in your pitch are your name, profession, and the problems you solve, the competitive advantages you possess, the ways people can learn more about your business, and who your ideal client is or might be.

See Tip #7 for taking the concept of an elevator pitch from basic to advanced in terms of networking strategy ... for now, use the "Notes" space at the end of this section to draft some answers to the basic questions I mentioned above.

T I P #2

REPEAT TIP #1!

 Seriously, develop and practice another pitch and keep going over and over until you master your ability to elevator pitch naturally, organically, and on-the-fly.

The goal is to be in command of different ways to communicate what you do and why you do it better than anyone else, all on your way to creating an interest in others wanting to work with you.

Now, use the "Notes" at the end of this section to draft a new set of answers to the basic questions you should answer in your pitch: your name, profession, and the problems you solve, the competitive advantages you possess, the ways people can learn more about your business, and who your ideal client is or might be.

T I P #3

LEARN AND MASTER
ACTIVE MARKETING SKILLS!

 Improve your listening by always seeking more information to listen to.

When someone is talking about themselves or their career/business, be ready to ask probing questions, qualifying questions, clarifying questions, or creative/hypothetical questions for the purpose of creating more "stuff" for you to listen to.

One of the most common remarks I receive in my client testimonials is that I took the time to really get to know the people I work with. Everyone will *say* they are all about helping others, but will anyone actually take the time to listen to their prospects deeply and strategically?

Preparing great questions is critical to show you really care through your ability and willingness to listen!

Again, more on the power of questions is coming in Tip #7, so for now get ready by using the "Notes" section to brainstorm/draft some questions you can ask in networking situations that will "give you more stuff to listen to?" Be creative ... be authentic ... be curious ... genuinely curious and eager to listen!

T I P #4

LOOK FOR SYNERGY!

 When an action serves more than one purpose that action represents a synergy for the two purposes along the lines of, "Feed two birds with one grain."

Don't just attend a networking event—consider the time and location of the event to see what ELSE you can attach to the networking event. Is there an errand you can run or a friend you can visit? Is there a business or prospect you can scout nearby the event? Is there someone you've been meaning to catch up with that might want to join you at the event?

Imagine a chess board ... now imagine if you are the chess player or a piece on the player's board? If all you do is attend a networking event, you are just a piece on the organizer's (not to mention the speaker's, sponsor's, host's/venue's, and other attendee's) boards.

If, however, attending a networking event is a piece on your board because you have intentionally attached other "moves" to attending the event, NOW you're the player!

Write down the next networking event you will attend, and THEN brainstorm ALL the other things you can "get done/achieve" in and around the attending of that event! Go!

TIP #5

LOOK FOR LEVERAGE!

 When you have a tool that gives you more power, you have leverage!

In the past, the classic networking tool was a business card because it simply gave us the power to be contacted by others if we have interested them in doing so—and an even more valuable power to contact others if we could get their card.

In the age of smartphones, there are apps and platforms you can acquire to give you more networking power. For example, a colleague owns a mobile marketing company that uses the power of text messaging. Subscribers to the service can have their clients text message a keyword to a five-digit number, and they will get an autoreply with a virtual business card or other marketing promotion/call to action.

T I P #6

POSITIONING IS POWER!

 Be strategic about your positioning when it comes to positioning as a form of leverage (See Tip #5 and imagine wrestling—the person on top usually has more leverage to score points and win the match).

How are you positioning yourself physically? That is simply about where you are in the room. Are you in front or in back ... in the middle or off to the side ... near the bar or near the stage ... in a position to meet the speaker, organizer or any VIP's ... standing up or sitting down ... attached at the hip to the same person all night long or moving throughout the people and space to maximize your exposure/opportunities.

Then, there's your verbal positioning ... how do you position yourself in terms of WHY you are at the event ... what you are hoping to achieve at the event ... who you are looking to meet at the event ... or to what degree you are intentional about helping others at the event?

Everything that comes out of your mouth puts you in SOME sort of position ... are you in a position of power, equality, neutrality, curiosity, service, persuasion, sponsorship, study/learning, expertise, or ignorance?

T I P #7

MASTER THESE 7 "REVERSIBLE QUESTIONS!"

 The exact words you use to ask these questions are not as important as understanding what you are REALLY asking (or being asked).

The following questions can be asked many different ways. Below is the question, followed by a second way it could be asked or how I might actually ask it myself when networking:

- What do you do? What is the greatest thing you do for people?

- Why do people choose you over your competition? What do you do better or different than other people who also do what you do?

- What are your tangible benefits? What do people "get" when they work with you?

- What are your emotional benefits? What do people "feel" when they work with you?

- How else could I learn more about you? How can you prove or back-up your answers to the first four questions?

- How does one qualify? What questions need to be answered to know if the relationship potential moving forward is "no, maybe, or YES?"

- Can I get your business card? Are we interested in following up with each other?

By making these questions reversible, I am calling attention to the fact that these are both great questions to ask people when you meet them, and these are the questions you will want to develop and practice multiple ways of responding to.

What will you say when you are asked any of the questions above? Working with the right coach will really help you nail this!

TIP #8

FOLLOW UP / THROUGH!

 Only a portion of the work of networking takes place during the events you attend. The rest of the work is done after the event! In fact, networking is worthless without follow-up and follow-through.

It is a great idea to have a pen handy to write notes onto business cards with keywords that may prompt the specific follow-up in order to build that relationship. Determine a system (like CRM or digital marketing platform) for processing contact info and business cards in ways that will remind and keep you accountable to follow-up and follow-through on the fieldwork of networking.

T I P #9

INTRODUCE YOURSELF TO THE VIP'S!

 The one person in the room likely to know 100% of everyone else in the room is the organizer!

Make sure the person that puts on an event knows you are there. Thank them for putting on the event and even ask if there is anything you can do to help with future events. Even if you already know the organizer, always announce yourself to them. Don't let it be taken for granted that you showed up ... make sure they know their event is something you support with the "gift" of showing up. They say showing up is "half the battle." Make sure the organizer knows that you showed up.

If the organizer is #1, then the guest speaker or special/featured guest of any kind (if there is one) is truly #1A. #1A is the person that the organizer leveraged to get you and others to show up to the event. Do your best to introduce yourself to them or ask a question if a Q&A session is opened. Wait in line if pictures are allowed. The work to befriend the guest speaker or special guest is always worth the effort.

Networking starts out as a quantity game (meet as many people as I can) and becomes a QUALITY game (meet the RIGHT people!). Identify the VIPs and do the WORK of positioning yourself to meet and interact with them!

T I P #10

LOVE!

 This rule is arguably #1 instead of #10 because if you love what you do and/or fall in love with what you do ... or love people or love helping people ... or love learning ... or love diversity ... or love love ... it will show on you.

You will have instant, raw, pure, and magnetic credibility when you LOVE what you are doing ... LOVE what you do ... LOVE what others do ... LOVE helping others do what they love ... LOVE connecting people that might end up LOVING each other ... LOVE being a person who LOVES! You get it?

I refer to M. Scott Peck (author of *The Road Less Traveled*) for my definition of LOVE, "The willingness to be vulnerable so that either you or your 'beloved' may grow!"

Make no mistake that we are vulnerable when we are networking, and it is our WILLINGNESS to be vulnerable that gives us our power to network—our power and willingness to grow and help others grow!

NOTES

Jeffrey Klubeck

SALES

DON'T ALWAYS BE CLOSING

Jeffrey Klubeck

I have always believed that "sales"
is a FIVE-letter word,
not a four-letter word.
Jeffrey Klubeck

Approach each customer with the idea of helping
him / her solve a problem or achieve a goal.
Brian Tracy

T I P #1

BUILD RAPPORT!

 In fact, do not do ANYTHING until you know you are in rapport with someone.

Building rapport is more than just noticing a picture in someone's office of them fishing and then saying you love fishing, too. Building rapport means a willingness to invest however much time it takes to really and truly get to know someone such that THEY feel, sense, or even declare that you do.

Don't confuse knowing someone with knowing everything about someone—that might never happen. Be very clear on the importance of your prospects believing that you have a good idea of who they are and how they got to be who they are.

When you do this work of getting to know someone in an honest and dedicated way, everything else you want to do in a sales process is much easier, including terminating the process when getting to know someone reveals that you should NOT be selling to them!

T I P #2

DIAGNOSE!

 Salespeople are not doctors, therapists, or psychiatrists ... per se, so maybe "discover" is a better and safer word than "diagnose."

Nonetheless, the tip here is to find out what needs to be different—what does the prospect want ... what do they REALLY want ... even better if you can find out WHY they want it and bonus points for figuring out how strongly they want it (see Tip #3). Or what is hurting them ... what is REALLY hurting them ... even better if you can find out WHY it is hurting them ... and, again, bonus points for figuring out how bad it hurts!

We are talking about pleasure and pain, the only two motivating forces on the planet. Does your product, service, investment, or experience/event get them out of that pain or closer to that pleasure? So many bad salespeople are leading with what I call "commission breath," which is what it smells like when you try to sell without taking the time to get clear about what the prospect wants/needs and why.

Last, you want the prospect to declare it themselves or agree with you when you say something like, "It sounds to me like you really want/need _____" is that right?" Of course, this step is so much easier if you have already done the work of Tip #1 (building rapport)!

T I P #3

GET LEVERAGE!

 Leverage, by definition, is the exertion of force by means of a lever or an object used in the manner of a lever … or the power to influence a person or situation to achieve a particular outcome.

Some of the most common levers used in sales are discounts, specials, bundles, and themed sales (like holidays sales or "everything must go" sales). Levers become more subtle in the forms of scarcity (for a limited time, or only 3 rooms left at this rate), exclusivity (be one of only 500 people to get this autographed jersey), or trial-ability/reciprocity, where you are given something for free which both serves the purpose of letting you try it risk free but also tapping the psychological aspect of guilt for getting something free that makes us want to give back or buy.

All of these are my least favorite forms of leverage compared to finding out HOW BAD the prospect really wants or needs to buy what you are selling. It goes back to Tip #2 in finding out what pleasure they seek or pain they wish to avoid. Once you have done that, leverage is getting the prospect to be super clear (like connected to the true emotional feelings) over how much it will hurt to stay in pain or go any longer without pleasure.

My favorite form of leverage is simply asking (to help the prospect SEE/FEEL) what have you missed or gone without or suffered through by not having _____ in the past … what is it costing you right now NOT to have _____ and if you don't get _____, what will it cost you in the future?

I have even asked entrepreneurs or struggling business owners if their spouse will leave them if they cannot get their business to be profitable. Is your marriage on the line if you don't make this business work? How much longer will your spouse tolerate being the sole income earner? How bad do you need business accountability in your life?

If you have built great rapport (tip #1) and accurately diagnosed their pleasure/pain status (tip #2) and been honest and real with them about what's at stake if they don't move forward (tip #3), you will have leverage to make sales that the most terrible salespeople never work hard enough to earn!

T I P #4

DROP THE SME!

 The step here is simply to demonstrate your Subject Matter Expertise (SME). The only real coaching for tip #4 is to really know your stuff! The more thoroughly you know exactly what you are selling, the more mastery you will have with this tip.

Rookie or just plain bad salespeople only learn their pitch, so it comes out the exact same way every single time—canned and with stinky "commission breath." However, your complete mastery of every detail of your product/service will allow you to highlight the exact features that match (solve) the prospects pleasure/pain relief seeking (benefits).

Therefore, this tip is to have MORE than one pitch—to have every possible pitch, so what you are pitching is calibrated to the specific pain/pleasure points you discovered in Tips 1-3 (Rapport, Diagnosis, Leverage). If you can customize your pitch to the needs of the prospect, you will achieve more sales.

One other key here is to present enough content/subject matter expertise and strategy to establish credibility in your knowledge and believability that you can meet their needs—but not SO MUCH that you fool them into thinking they do not need to move forward with the purchase/investment.

Have you ever seen a movie trailer and immediately afterward said to yourself or out loud, "Well, I don't need to see that movie now…" believing that the trailer had already shown you everything and/or the res" was either predictable or not worth the investment? Yeah, well, don't do that with your stuff!

NO whiteboard is safe when
Klubeck is onsite to share his SME!

T I P #5

KNOW YOUR 1, 2, 3's!

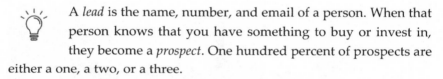 A *lead* is the name, number, and email of a person. When that person knows that you have something to buy or invest in, they become a *prospect*. One hundred percent of prospects are either a one, a two, or a three.

A "1" is a buyer! They are ready to buy now! Right now! They have zero concerns that need to be addressed … they have a credit card in hand … they know they want to buy, they showed up or called in so they could buy, and your job is to sell them as much as you can that still makes sense for them! Hint: Have a VIP package already created for the rare occurrence that you are selling to a "1."

A "2" is a potential buyer. They are ready to buy now … but! It's the "but," all the "buts," every single "but" that equals a concern they will need you to address before they are able to buy. Unlike the #1 (sell as much as you can,) your goal is to identify and address all of their concerns. If you can do that, you will get a yes to something … even if it is only permission to follow up with them in an agreed upon time frame, you have gotten a yes! A yes is every bit as important as an actual sale because all yeses lead to sales at some point.

You might have a $5,000 VIP package … sell that to your #1 and start with your $100 entry level package for a #2, but ONLY after you have identified and addressed all of their concerns. Once they say "yes" to the littlest thing, it's a sign of trust and then your products/services can do the rest in terms of "wowing" them to upsells and repeat business.

If you treat a #2 like a #1 or a #3, you could be making a big mistake! That brings us to #3s which are the non-buyers … plain and simple. They are not buying. They are still not buying … and they will NEVER buy. The sooner you identify a prospect as a #3, the sooner you can terminate the sales process and save time for your #1's and #2's. Trying to convince a #3 that they are a #2 or a #1 is like shooting yourself in the foot with a gun before trying to win the 100-yard dash! Sometimes a #3 will disguise themselves as a #2 or a #1 showing enough interest to get free information or products or samples. Or they may even be a plant from the competitor who is on assignment to study your sales process, products, and pricing. So, KNOW your 1, 2, 3's when it comes to sales and have a plan to identify who is who as soon in your sales process as possible!

T I P #6

DEVELOP MULTIPLE CALLS TO ACTION!

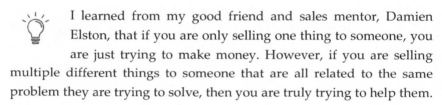 I learned from my good friend and sales mentor, Damien Elston, that if you are only selling one thing to someone, you are just trying to make money. However, if you are selling multiple different things to someone that are all related to the same problem they are trying to solve, then you are truly trying to help them.

Damien gives a great example of how selling only protein powder will not get someone in lean shape. That person will also need many other things to achieve their goal, such as a bottle to shake it in, a nutrition plan, an exercise plan, and other ingredients for shake-making.

Moreover, as we discussed in Tip #5, some people will be ready for your VIP package right away and others might start out at entry level. Some people in Vegas like to play the $5 tables and some people like to play the $500 tables. The point is Las Vegas has options for people at every price point from penny and nickel slots to $50,000 minimum bets. So, do you? Do you have a predetermined option for any scenario to increase the chances of getting a new customer, sale, or positive step by a prospect in that direction?

As I write this tip, I am on the verge of creating info products for online delivery at every price level. I want to have a $7 course, a $17 course, a $47, $97, $147, $197, $297, $497, $797, $997, and so on. I want everyone that knows anything about me to be able to try my "stuff" in hopes they will think it's valuable and then buy more.

Remember, someone that just clicks an online ad may not see me as credible as someone that saw me speak live for 90 minutes. Therefore, I need different calls to action for each scenario to increase my yes/conversion rates. If I only have one action that people can take to engage with my "stuff," then I will do less sales.

Constantly innovate new ways to package your solutions. Brainstorm new actions you can encourage your prospects to take toward becoming buyers, including actual purchases, by having many options for the diversity of concerns or budgets your prospects may have.

T I P #7

KISS!

Keep It Simple Salesperson! ☺

What you need to understand here is that a confused mind will not buy. Confusion is one of the strongest barriers to moving forward with a purchase/investment while it is one of the easiest concerns to avoid in the first place! If you can practice NEVER saying anything that might confuse the buyer then they will never be confused.

A common mistake that bad salespeople make is talking oneself out of a sale by continuing to share information that has not been requested by the prospect. The bad salesperson is trying to earn the right to ask for the sale by showing you everything ... going over all the bells, whistles, features, etc. They run the risk of boring or confusing you with information that may not be of interest to you.

Whereas you must make your knowledge of your "stuff" work for you in a sales presentation, you must also avoid the curse of knowledge which is when you have actually forgotten what it is like NOT to know what you know. When that happens, you might be explaining things in terms the prospect doesn't understand, but now you have taken for granted because of your expertise.

Practice only sharing information that the customer has asked for and asking "check-in" questions such as, "Did that answer your question?" or "Does that make sense to you?" or "Would you like me to elaborate or explain any further or did you have another question I can answer?"

Keeping it simple and *matching the knowledge pace* of the prospect will definitely lead to an increase in sales!

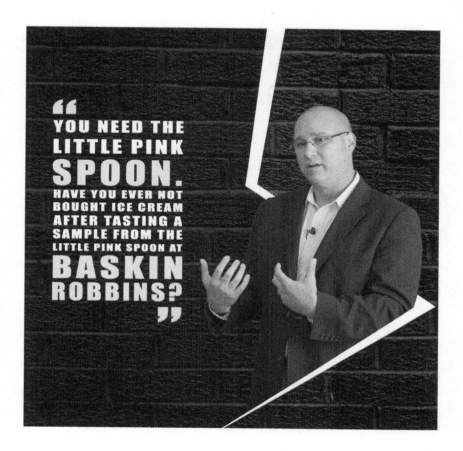

T I P #8

UNDERSTAND DISC / MOTIVATORS!

 I could have said "Understand Behavioral Styles/Pursuits" ... but I chose to say DISC/Motivators because those are the names of the assessments I conduct for all new clients.

The Motivators Assessment lets me know what someone feels life is the pursuit of ... what gets them out of bed or off the couch ... and what meaning they make of the world around them.

The DISC, on the other hand, tells me the emotional charge behind someone's behavioral style—if they are intense or passive, optimistic or pessimistic, fast- paced or slow to change, detailed/analytical or stubborn/rebellious. There are over 3,000 different psychometric assessments (often known as personality tests), and my go-to are the DISC combined with the Motivators.

Selling to an analytical person requires a different approach than selling to a persuasive person. Selling to a direct person is different than selling to a supportive person. Selling to someone that wants to control the conversation is different than selling to someone that wants a traditional or informative experience.

Being able to read behavioral motivators and styles combined with an ability to adapt your own instinctual style to match the style of the prospect will lead to more sales.

T I P #9

TRUE SALESFORCE!

 I believe you have a TRUE salesforce when you have people who are NOT on payroll selling for you. There are a couple of ways you can do this.

First and foremost, make sure your customers are continuously blown-away with value, service, selection, and special care. It is so much harder to get a new client than it is to keep a happy one ... and happy clients usually refer people to you.

Dr. Nido Quebin talks about levels of branding that starts at awareness and progresses to preference, insistence, and finally advocacy where the customer/client not ONLY insists on buying from you for themselves, but also insists that others (friends, family, strangers on the subway, etc.) do, as well.

Another way to create a true salesforce, is to find other people that ALSO sell to your target prospects and "white label" your services so they can profit if they sell you to their customers. Sometimes this takes the form of affiliate relationships and joint ventures. I conduct behavioral assessments, which makes me the "assessment guy" for other organizations that know the value of assessments but don't sell or conduct them on their own. Shout out to my friends at Workplace Training Network, Orange Leaf Consulting, Wolf Management Consultants, and EYE Coaching and Consulting—all of whom look to me when they have clients needing Assessment Solutions.

The classic networking group that does about as good a job as can be done with Tip #9 is BNI (Business Networking International). There are always drawbacks to any networking group, but I believe BNI has systematized the process of turning your networking group members into an extended sales force for your business. Founder Ivan Misner has written many books of the power and strategies of professional networking and expanding your informal (non-payroll) salesforce.

Klubeck with colleague Brian Traichel and
BNI Founder Ivan Misner in 2009.

T I P #10

READING ISN'T ENOUGH!

 Be clear, reading about sales is MANDATORY if you want to be great at sales ... and but equally clear that reading is NOT enough to be great. You must also get training ... constantly ... several times a year, if possible.

Putting yourself into a live sales training environment forces you to act out what you learn. If the training is any good, it will force you to speak, to role play, and to create dialogues and product trees.

A great sales training will have a combination of instruction and coaching to support your learning and growth or transformation from a behavioral perspective.

A great sales training will address any mindset issues you may be bringing to the sale. A great sales training might provide video recording of your role plays and presentations.

A great sales training will be led by people who LOVE sales and have mastered sales with over 10,000 hours (to reference Malcom Gladwell's standard).

A great sales training will break down what you are doing well, poorly, not doing at all, and should not be doing at all.

And that same great training will build you back up with the ability to execute sales mastery (storytelling, concern-addressing, rapport-building, diagnosis, pre-qualifying, trial-closing, emotionally connecting, attention-getting, leveraging, seed-planting, closing/moving people to action, and more!!!).

Contact me if you want to learn how you can attend the best sales training I have ever experienced! It has everything above and more!

NOTES

ACCOUNTABILITY

"NOTHING IS INSURMOUNTABLE WHEN I'M HUGGING YOU ACCOUNTABLE."
Coach Jeffrey

It would be easy to understand and deliver accountability as "bad cop" coaching ... However, a world-class accountability coach delivers accountability with permission first, and love always.
Jeffrey Klubeck

It is wrong and immoral to seek to escape the consequences of one's acts.
Mahatma Gandhi

T I P #1

LOOK WITHIN!

 Hey, pot, you're black! It takes one to know one! Do you see where this is going? Yeah, you!

Accountability (like integrity, parenting, or driving) is a term that is most often used when someone is accusing someone else of being poor at it, as if they themselves are fine/perfect. I believe we are always guilty of what we accuse others of and one of the reasons it is so easy to notice a lack of accountability in others is because of how much room we have to improve our own. It's always easier to accuse others than look within. So, as one of my mentors Brian Tracy would say, "Eat That Frog!" and make the hardest thing to do (looking within) your number 1 priority when it comes to improving your ability to hold others accountable—it starts with our own accountability.

Question: Who holds you accountable? Don't answer until you have read the rest of the tips because a lot of people think they know what accountability is when they don't ... think they are accountable when they are not ... think they are HELD accountable when they are not.

For now, Tip #1, accept that the road to greater accountability in your life and especially the performance of those that report to you (or your clients) is paved with your own vulnerability—your own willingness to be held accountable—to be pushed, confronted, challenged, questioned, probed, motivated, and celebrated the way a world-class accountability coach provides that level of support.

Much the same way you cannot love others unless you love yourself, you cannot hold others accountable unless you have the experience in your own life of being held accountable. The question of what we are being held accountable to is a different matter entirely!

T I P #2

UNDERSTAND INTEGRITY!

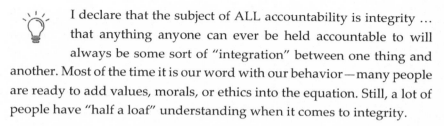 I declare that the subject of ALL accountability is integrity ... that anything anyone can ever be held accountable to will always be some sort of "integration" between one thing and another. Most of the time it is our word with our behavior—many people are ready to add values, morals, or ethics into the equation. Still, a lot of people have "half a loaf" understanding when it comes to integrity.

When I am training independent coaches and managers/directors of organizations, I am always teaching people to focus on the word "integration" when it comes to an understanding of integrity—where one thing comes together with another thing.

In developing my coaching/leadership training program, I developed a 10-point model of integrity. When I present it in a public speaking situation (like a business retreat, coaches training, or keynote), I always begin by asking the audience, "How many of you understand what integrity is?" and someone helps me establish what I covered above (the coming together of one thing with another). Then I'll ask, "How many believe you have great integrity?" Everyone in the room raises their hand. Then I politely request that they NOT shoot the messenger as I present "The Klubeck 10-Step" Model of Integrity. Meaning, here are the 10 things I help my clients discover and integrate ...so that the largest percentage of our daily activities feed these 10 points in question form:

- **Meaning with Purpose:** Have you discovered or decided on what you believe to be a "meaning of life" and have you discovered or decided what you believe to be YOUR life's purpose? Are they integrated? Is there a clear connection between your meaning of life and the meaning of YOUR life?

- **Purpose with Gifts:** Do you believe, as I do, that all human beings are gifted, and have you decided or discovered what YOUR gifts are? Is there integration (a clear relationship) between your life's purpose and the gifts you've been given? Are you applying your gifts for hobby, pastime, playtime, or mission/service/purpose?

- **Gifts with Potential:** Have you discovered or decided what your potential is based on the gifts you have been given? Have you attempted to calculate what measurable results you can achieve … how fast you can get … how many people you can teach … how many books you can sell … how many mouths you can feed … how many kids you can put through school … how many businesses you can start … how high up in the company you can get? Have you declared what you are capable of achieving in the long term based on your gifts? Is there a relationship between your gifts and your potential? You bet there is!

- **Potential with Goals:** First of all, do you set goals? Chances are the answer is no because the Ivy League studies all conclude that only about 3% of our population sets goals. Secondly, if you DID set goals, would those goals be based on what you see other people achieving or would your goals be INTEGRATED with YOUR potential based on YOUR gifts (versus what the Kardashians are doing, for example.)? So many people are trying to achieve what others expect of them or what they see others doing instead of looking within at the factors above and putting themselves in a position to be held accountable to integrity, but we're not done…

- **Goals with Strategy/Tactics:** Do you have strategies to choose from that will help you achieve your goals? Are the strategies you are considering integrated with the goals you want to achieve (if your goal is to increase sales and your strategy is to pray, I'm not sure there is ideal integration there. But if your strategy was to knock on doors and make phone calls, I think there would be more integration there)? Moreover, since there is more than one way to get a job done, are you considering strategies that are difficult or natural for someone (integrated) with your gifts?

- **Strategy/Tactics with Word/Commitment:** Have you selected a strategy and broken it down into the tactics (observable actions you need to take to execute the strategy), AND are you committed to taking that action? To whom, if anyone, have you shared that commitment … given your word? What is your relationship with your word? Most people know that integrity has something to do with doing what you say you will do. So what percentage of the things you say you will do, do you actually do? And what percentage of the things you say you will do are integrated with a strategy or what you would call "strategic?" Legendary basketball coach John Wooden cautioned us not to mistake activity with achievement. Most people are really good at staying busy but what percentage of our day-to-day activities are things we said we would do, or strategic or advancing us toward our goals (which we probably haven't set) or our potential (which we probably haven't determined) or our purpose (which we are probably too busy to discover or too scared to acknowledge … because as soon as we do, we can be held accountable … I digress). Still not done!

- **Word/Commitment with Action:** I kind of covered this at the end of the last point—are you making commitments to take strategic action toward SMAART Goals (more on SMAART in Tip #3), and are you actually taking that action? Are you putting-off or delaying the difficult things that you know will make the difference? If we all did 100 things every day, how many of those

100 would be things we committed to doing … things we said to ourselves or to another that we would do? Most people offer a number less than 50% when I ask this question at my events. So, 35% of the things we do are things we said we would do … but how many of the things we say we will do are tactics that execute a proven strategy for a specific goal? Now imagine me asking an audience to, "Raise your hand if you feel you have great integrity now?" Remember: please don't shoot the messenger; I'm not done.

- **Action with Growth:** Are you taking enough action to make mistakes? I ask because there is no such thing as a mistake—just learning and growth wrapped in a little discomfort. In fact, the only mistake to be afraid of is the one you don't learn from. Most people are so afraid of mistakes and failure that they never take action towards their goals as I've outlined above. So, I ask: are the actions you are taking integrated with your personal/ professional/financial/spiritual growth?

- **Growth with Achievements:** Straightforwardly, what are your achievements? Do you have any at all? Are they positive achievements or negative achievements? Getting locked up in jail eight times in eight years, for example, IS an achievement, but not one that is integrated with growth! What are your achievements and are they "integrated" (related) with the growth you experienced because you KNOW what you want and have COMMITTED to getting it? **And finally…**

- **Achievements with Contributions:** In our last point of integration, we "integrate" (come full circle) with the first point (meaning and purpose) when asking: what are you doing with your achievements … who are you sharing them with … who are you giving to … whose life are you touching with contribution … are you doing something that helps your family … that helps your community … that helps humanity? Is there integration between what you are achieving and who you are serving … who you are contributing to? Are the contributions you are making to this world integrated with what you believe to be the meaning of life and your specific life's purpose? Do you know your gifts, potential, goals, ideal strategies, capacity to commit, power of action, joy of growing pain, the responsibility of achievement and the pure gift of contribution?

Ker-plunk (mic-drop). Seriously, most people are comfortable accusing other people of not having integrity when we ALL have room to improve ... hopefully, that's easier to see/admit when we look at the 10-point model above. Consider Get A Klu's 2 Complimentary Coaching Sessions (apply at www.getaklu.net) to work with a coach on helping you discover and declare your purpose, gifts, potential, and goals!

T I P #3

GET S.M.A.A.R.T. ABOUT GOAL SETTING!

 As with integrity, when asked, most people will tell you that they set goals.

This is because they are confusing a hope, wish, dream (macro) or a task, activity, or commitment (micro) with a goal. Second, most people are unaware how vast the studies are that have been conducted on high-achieving individuals that reveal 100% of them to share the habit of goal setting, but also tell us that only 3% of the population sets goals.

When I speak and train clients on goal setting, I make sure people understand the five reasons why we fail to set goals, and one of those is that we don't know how. I personally never learned how to set goals in school, which was bad enough, but then when I finally did learn about goals during my coaches training education, I learned to make goals S.M.A.R.T. (specific, measurable, achievable, realistic, and time-bound), in turn, making them accountable. I was thrilled!

What a difference when we add "specific, measurable, and time-bound" as criteria to what we want—that's the difference between a hope, wish, dream, and a GOAL: a specific and measurable "what" happens by a specific time-bound "when."

But there's more to the model (the "A" and the "R") and soon into building my own coaching practice, I realized there was something stupid about S.M.A.R.T. ... just kidding ... I mean, there was something redundant and a couple things missing. Let me explain...

The original "A" is for "achievable or attainable" and one way to know that our goals are achievable is if we *believe* we can achieve them. Belief is a feeling of certainty that something is true ... so if we believe we can do it then that becomes our reality: we can do it! Therefore, if the goal is achievable (we believe we can and that's our reality) then it is also realistic (to us) and that makes the "R" in S.M.A.R.T. redundant.

Are you tracking? When I am helping clients set goals, I hold them accountable to ONLY setting a goal they truly believe they can achieve—not the goal they know they are going to achieve no matter what, but the one they know the CAN achieve even if it will be difficult or require effort! Hold that thought ...(Visit www.theklubrary.com for free and for-pay content, including real life samples of me coaching people on goal setting). Meanwhile...

Another problem I saw in the model were two things I felt were missing: 1) ambition/will-power and 2) motivation or the "why" of the goal! Meaning, with the original S.M.A.R.T. criteria, someone could set a goal to achieve something predictable, or that they are already going to achieve anyway and think it's a goal. Meaning, someone could set a goal that meets the S.M.A.R.T. criteria without having to change behavior. Someone could technically set a goal of brushing their teeth twice a day for 30 days straight—something they are likely to do anyway whether they call it a goal or not.

In the coaching business, we are interested in helping people get results they DON'T already have, which means they need to change behavior in some way, and if so, then their goal is ambitious. The second "A" in my model is for the "ambition" it takes to decrease, increase, start, or stop a behavior, but doing the same thing over and over expecting different results, as we all know, is insanity! So, when it comes to goal setting, make sure you are aware of a behavior that needs to change in order for the goal to be achieved ... or it's not really a goal, is it?

What about the "R" then? The original S.M.A.R.T. model uses "R" for realistic, which I think is redundant, but also leaves "why" or "motivation" out of the model. So, I changed the "R" from realistic (which we established is covered by "achievable") to "reason/reward," because, in the words of Simon Sinek, it is critical to "Know Your Why?" When I work with my coaching clients to set goals, I hold them accountable to declaring as much "WHY they want the goal" as possible. (Visit www.theklubrary.com for free and affordable e-sources and e-courses.) They need to have more reasons to want to achieve the goal than to give up on or procrastinate on it. If we have just one reason for doing something, we might get around to doing it. But if we are clear on five or six reasons why we want something, we might be unstoppable and certainly more willing to be held accountable!

I would like to think I have made S.M.A.R.T. even S.M.A.A.R.T.er ... and to make it even S.M.A.A.R.T.E.R. you add the "E" for evaluate ... and the second "R" for revise. My mom taught me that humans plan and God laughs. Therefore, it is important to periodically check in on the progress you are making or make room for unexpected life events that occur and evaluate/revise your goals to make sure they are always achievable and relevant.

If you'd like to get S.M.A.A.R.T. about your own goal setting, consider sessions with a Get A Klu coach or the self-paced e-course on SMAART Goal Setting I recorded. (Visit www.theklubrary.com for free and affordable e-sources and e-courses.) Learn it! Live it!

Klubeck loves conducting Goal-Setting Workshops where
NO whiteboard is safe!

TIP #4

LOOK OUTSIDE!

In Accountability Tip #1, we asked you to "Look Within!" and find whatever humility or courage or desperation or desire it will take to be willing to be held accountable. Now, in Tip #4, we are suggesting you look outside yourself for that accountability.

This tip, or all of my top 10 tips, (or even a Certificate of Completion from my Coaching/Leadership Training) will make you better at holding yourself accountable, but none of us will ever be as good at it as someone else will. And, let me be clear that I mean someone trained with the tools, techniques, skill sets and experience to hold you accountable.

Many people try to turn their friends into "accountability partners" because it sounds good in the moment, or because they don't want to pay for coaching. These arrangements rarely last because:

- Neither of you have skin in the game (money invested) which means both of you are likely to cancel, postpone, or delay your accountabilities believing there is no immediate consequence.

- The social graces of friendship are in conflict with the demands of confrontation and accountability. Neither of you are conditioned to upset each other or "risk" the friendship with any firm position on an issue or confrontation on a behavior. If a friend says, "I can't do it today," the other friend is WAY more likely to just say "Okay" than to confront the "why" of not doing and truly hold the person accountable to the viability of keeping/breaking their commitment. Mere friends are not training to handle the accountability side of that, only the "keep the friendship" side.

- Friends may love you, but love alone does not qualify someone to effectively hold another accountable. I say that as someone who went through countless hours of accountability training and practice with my own clients and coaches. In the Get A Klu approach to accountability, love is necessary, but not sufficient!

- So, it's not just "look outside" for external accountability, but make sure you are looking for a trained, skilled, experienced, or, dare I say, professional, source of accountability!

TIP #5

SECURE PERMISSION!

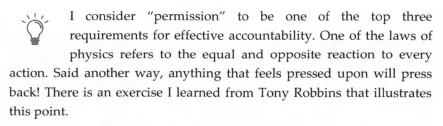 I consider "permission" to be one of the top three requirements for effective accountability. One of the laws of physics refers to the equal and opposite reaction to every action. Said another way, anything that feels pressed upon will press back! There is an exercise I learned from Tony Robbins that illustrates this point.

Put your hands together palm to palm. On the count of 3, press as hard as you can onto your weaker hand with your stronger hand. Don't cheat—wait until the count of 3.

Are you ready? 1…2…3! Press as hard as you can! Harder! Are your hands still in front of or nearly in front of your face? I didn't say press BACK!

Do you understand? You actively sent a message to your stronger hand to press, but do you recall TELLING your other hand to resist? No. Resistance was automatic! The laws of physics tell us that the reaction will be equal and opposite, but it fails to highlight the automatic part. It's automatic to press back when pressed upon.

When it comes to accountability you have to expect, anticipate, plan for, prepare for, and be skilled at dealing with this "automatic, equal and opposite" reaction to your efforts to hold people accountable—to your actions of confrontation. Expect pushback unless permission is secured first.

When you have permission to confront ... permission to account ... permission to suggest ... permission to explain ... permission to tell a story, etc. When you have that permission, your efforts are PART of that permission vs. counter to it. Your accountability is an extension of permission vs. a provocation of push back.

Get A Klu's Coaching/Leadership Training teaches you dozens of techniques to secure the permission you need to avoid the pushback that prevents true accountability.

T I P #6

AUTHORING STATE OF MIND!

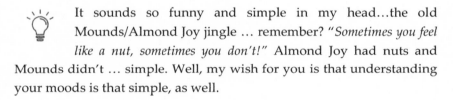 It sounds so funny and simple in my head…the old Mounds/Almond Joy jingle … remember? *"Sometimes you feel like a nut, sometimes you don't!"* Almond Joy had nuts and Mounds didn't … simple. Well, my wish for you is that understanding your moods is that simple, as well.

"Sometimes our mood is a reaction, sometimes it's NOT!" It is a truth that for most of us most of the time, the mood that we are in is a response to stimuli that is determined by our past experiences and understandings of pleasure, pain, good, bad, right, wrong, etc.

Another truth is that at ANY time, we have the ability to decide what mood we PREFER to be in and actually (we have the ability to) generate that mood at any given time. "Generate," you say? Yeah, here are the synonyms I could have used: author, create, manufacture, cook, create, bring forth, assume, produce, etc. Get the idea?

Many people want to be victims and helpless when it comes to explaining why they don't have what they want or why they can't get what they want, and the truth is that it's all bull shit! Viktor Frankel, in his book *Man's Search for Meaning,* taught us that NOBODY can EVER take away from us our ability to decide what things MEAN!

Meaning making is synonymous with "mood authoring," and when you realize that the mood we are in is ALWAYS the pre-determinant of our decisions regarding actions and behaviors, you'd realize how valuable it is to AUTHOR your state of mind, to author your moods, and take greater control over the meaning you make of the events and experiences you encounter. A world-class coach will hold you accountable to making meanings that serve you vs. otherwise. A world-class coach can explain to you exactly how to "author your state of mind" by manipulating three things:

- **Your language choice/pattern**

- **Your physiology regarding posture, movement, and biochemistry**

- **Your beliefs of choice in any given moment**

Tony Robbins refers to these three ingredients as a TRIAD, and I am a big fan of replacing negative with positive TRIADS. It is a special skill set to develop and master because it changes lives! I have worked hard at it since 2007 helping people with their mindset in over 12 countries and many major cities within those countries. It is so rewarding to help people get out of their own way!

Jeffrey Klubeck and his family in Australia

However, this is not the place to train you on what I call the "psycho-surgical skill-set of TRIAD Transplant." My goal here is to "daylight" mindset and our ability to author our moods in any given moment. This is something we all should be held accountable for. If you are not holding someone accountable for empowering meaning-making and mood-setting, you are failing as an accountability coach/leader.

T I P #7

GATHER TOOLS OF CONFRONTATION!

 I am leading off this tip with one of those universal laws that we have probably all heard about and all understand on at least some level: *every action has an equal and opposite reaction.*

What does that mean regarding our efforts to confront and account for our client's (direct report's) behavior? If each action has an equal and opposite reaction, then what will happen when we ask someone if they did what they said they would do ... what they were supposed to do ... what is best for them to do ... what we know will get them the result they seek?

Will they just ask us the exact same questions and push back with "equal and opposite reaction" to being confronted or pressed-upon for accountability? Not if we use certain tools of confrontation that align us with the client in a way that they see us as part of themselves vs. an adversarial force. May I share just a few of these tools and hope that you wish to learn more about them and others in our coaching and leadership training? Thank you:

- **Levels of Posture:** Sometimes we need to shift our posture with our clients/direct reports to keep them off balance enough that the reaction cannot be equal and opposite. Sometimes we must take an inferior posture, other times a superior posture, and other times an equal posture during the coaching session dialogue and process of confronting someone who is out of integrity on their commitments.

- **Range of Emotional Engagement:** The martial arts analogy applies here when we think about range and the distance from us that another person is physically: kicking range, punching range, trapping range, and grappling range! Each range represents an increase in closeness of one person with another, which, in turn, represents an increase in techniques that can be applied to the person. The same holds true for emotional engagement when we use stories, open sharing, excellent questions and our own vulnerabilities in order to draw our clients/direct reports closer to us emotionally — paving the way for them to share and receive more openly which in turn paves the way for "collaborative" vs. "adversarial" accountability — and that doesn't get pressed back upon!

- **Aristotle's "Ingredients of Persuasion:"** You have probably heard of these referred to as logos, ethos, and pathos. Do you remember which is which? That's okay ... let me help.

The way to remember logos is logic. The LOG. Logic refers to "the argument" — what are you arguing? Of all the arguments you could make they will all be one of three kinds! You are either arguing that *something is a fact,* or you are arguing that we *perceive a value* of something, or you are arguing that *we behave (or refrain from behaving) in a certain way.* Fact, value, policy!

We make our arguments more believable and acceptable if we provide congruent evidence and reasoning. Any of these three ingredients (claim, evidence, reasoning) that do not follow from one another equals a FALLACY! Beware of fallacies ... so many 100-level college courses address the nature of fallacies and make the educated aware of dangerous argument patterns. So, when you understand argumentation and the difference between sound and flawed logic, you are in a better position to hold someone accountable.

The way to remember ethos is ethics. The ETH. Ethics refers to the credibility of the arguer, not necessarily the argument. Ethos/Ethics answers the questions: What makes you credible to make that argument? How do you know what you know? What are your sources? There is a certain amount of credibility required to escape the consequences of accountability and there is perhaps even more credibility required to apply the forces and consequences of accountability. Be clear, that credibility is an important factor in accountability!

The way to remember pathos is pathological. The PATH. I consider myself an empath, which means I can feel what other people feel. When we are talking about feelings, we are talking about emotions—and pathos is an ability to appeal to the emotions of the person you wish to persuade.

A world-class coach MUST understand the dominant emotions that drive human psychology such as: safety, certainty, belonging, excitement, esteem, connection, growth, and contribution.

From Aristotle to Abraham Maslow to Karl Jung to Tony Robbins and beyond, the emotions that drive our behavior, the emotions we actually become addicted to, those drivers of our inner psychology have been well studied and can be appealed to in the course increasing the chances our subjects will do what they say they will do!

There are more tools of confrontation you could learn about, and I would love to see you enroll in our trainings. For now, understand that it will be difficult to confront someone without being ready for, if not totally pre-empting, the equal and opposite reaction that human beings will display when being pressed upon.

T I P #8

FIND A WAY TO LOVE!

 One great irony of accountability, in general, and especially within a coaching/direct report conversation, is the sizzle (packaging) vs. the steak (substance) of it.

On the surface, accountability is a word/concept that we associate with terms such as confrontation, reporting, admitting, judgment, and even punishment or consequence (to speak only of the negative in this case.) Because those are all things that most people wish to avoid, a lack of accountability is arguably the single greatest epidemic to personal and professional productivity—the ultimate threat to an individual or organization's potential.

And it hurts to some degree, at least in my work where I see SUCH a lack of accountability and get paid quite well to install mindsets and cultures of accountability into leaders and organizations. It hurts to see so much potential being unmet and so much time, energy, and money wasted due to how hard people work to avoid being accountable.

Yet, here's the irony ... accountability actually requires love ... yeah, I said it ... LOVE! First of all, ask yourself what kind of person would work HARD to avoid LOVE or being loved? Second, let me explain...

I believe you will find no better definition for the word "love" than what was offered to us by Dr. M. Scott Peck in his classic work, *The Road Less Traveled:* "The willingness to be vulnerable for either your own or another's spiritual [personal/professional] growth." Peck's definition uses the word "spiritual" in front of growth, I added [personal/professional] because they are forms of growth requiring vulnerability—not because they lead to or equate to the power of spiritual growth (another topic for another time).

Because of all that packaging associated with accountability (and knowing how much ourselves and others avoid being accountable and how hard we will work to avoid it,) imagine how much you have to care about someone or the organization in order to hold someone accountable—to confront, challenge, question, count, measure, or verify someone else's behavior and results—to take the effort to do that knowing of the negative connotations and how hard people work to avoid it. That takes some kind of courage ... some kind of "care" ... some kind of "vulnerability" to the push back ... the denials ... the preemptive accusations ... the politics ... the YOU NAME IT (and we've all seen the ugly reactions people can have when being held accountable. In fact, part of the strategy to AVOID it happening again is to throw such a tantrum that the other persons just says, "It's not worth it" and fails to confront). Are you following me?

I will ONLY hold you accountable and risk the elusiveness, the push-back, the smoke and mirrors, the slipping and sliding, the excuses, the unreturned phone calls, the "I forgots" and "I can't find its," and the "It wasn't my faults" (and everything else I get when confronting), I brave it ALL for the purpose of my clients personal/professional/spiritual growth! If I don't love you, care for you, cheer for your growth and potential actualized, then I don't count ... I don't confront ... I don't ask ... I don't question ... I don't support ... I don't lead ... and I don't love!

Leadership ... Accountability ... Confrontation ... it's all LOVE! See it that way and you might be on your way to a little more accountability in your life!

TIP #9

STOP CALLING IT TIME MANAGEMENT!

The number one strategy for time management is to set goals. If you do a great job with goal setting, you will make better decisions about what you do "in time." Beyond that, you need to STOP calling it "time management" for some very important reasons.

- Time manages itself … quite well, in fact. I encourage you to read a book by a future friend of mine, Mitch Albom, called *The Timekeeper*. The book is about a curse bestowed upon the first person to ever attempt to measure (control/manage) time. It is a tremendous read that will change your perspectives on time all together. My suggestion here is to simply be humble and honest and to admit that we do not manage time — that time is a concept far beyond us and totally automated with no help from us humans.

- Second, what CAN we manage? Ourselves! Our moods, our decisions, our actions, all of which occur in time, but can you see how the focus shifts towards accountability when we get honest about what we truly CAN manage? I love public speaking on this topic when I ask people to repeat after me if they have ever said out loud the things I say out loud, like, "I don't have time"… "If only "there were more time"… "I ran out of time"… "I don't have self"…gotcha! You never say that last one! "If only there were more tasks"… "I ran out of purpose"… "If only there were more discipline in the day"…do you see what I'm getting at? When we look within at what we CAN control, we can be accountable…so most people call it time management as if it is the fault of time that we are underachieving.

- Finally, when we say "I need better time management" we have a victim mindset. Were we to say instead, "I need better decision management or self-management … or task management … or calendar management … or purpose/priority management," we would be demonstrating an "accountable mindset." Stay accountable, my friends!

T I P #10

ASK QUESTIONS!

 The first paragraph here also shows up in Tip #4 of my Top 10 Communication tips overall … and the rest I have to say about questions are specific to accountability vs. communication or relationships as a whole.

Better yet, become a master at asking questions! Did you know that a human brain, once hearing a question will always attempt to answer it? That's powerful because it means that questions are among the most powerful in a category of communication techniques called "attention getters." Simply put, when you have someone's attention, communication is easier…

… and when it comes to accountability, even the most permission-based and loving confrontation is much easier when you have someone's attention. One key to all of this is how much more likely a statement is to provoke a defensive response than a question is. When possible, ALWAYS replace statements with questions! As an example, allow me to provide a "stream of consciousness" list of questions I might ask a client in the context of holding them accountability to committing to the actions that will accelerate their progress and then making sure they DO what they say they are going to do … enjoy:

- Did you say you are committed to that action?

- Is that something you are just committed to accomplish by yourself or is that something you want me to hold you accountable for?

- Would you like "front end" accountability?

- How long will it take you to complete that action?

- When is the soonest availability you have to complete that action?

- What are you doing in between now and then that is MORE important to your GOALS than THIS action? Why is that important? Which of those two things is REALLY more important?

- Are you comfortable pushing this off until then, or can you reschedule the less important to prioritize the more important?

- What are you going to do when you hang up the phone? And after that? And after that?

- When is the SOONEST you can possibly complete the action we are talking about here?

- Would you like "between session" accountability?

- Would it help if you committed to letting me know as SOON as you complete this action by text, email, or phone? Smoke screen, S.O.S., pigeon carrier, message in a bottle, Morse Code, Pony Express ... anything?

- Would it help to say, "Take THAT Coach!" in your message when you notify me upon completion?

- Do you want me to set a reminder in my calendar and phone to REMIND YOU to complete this action? If so, how soon BEFORE your appointment with yourself would you like to be reminded?

- How will we know that this got done? What will be observable after you do this that is not observable now? How could I observe that?

- Or are you comfortable with the power of your word that you'll complete this, and I won't ask you about it until the "back end" (next session)?

- Would you like me to trust that you'll get this done by the next time we talk, or would you like to make an AWS on your calendar and invite me to "attend," so it shows up on my calendar?
- What is a consequence you wish to avoid that you can COMMIT TO SUFFERING if you fail to complete this action?
- What is a great REWARD you can give yourself for completing this action?

I could go on and on because I love coming up with different questions that deliver the ingredients of accountability in permission-seeking ways! I like that: **Get A Klu** coaches use permission-seeking tactics to deliver the ingredients of powerful accountability! Do you like that?

That concludes my Top 10 Tips on Accountability. The truth is there is SO MUCH more to learn on this topic, especially for the person wanting to become a coach, the coach wanting to become a better coach, the struggling coach needing to provide just a bit more value in order to enroll more coaching clients, or the supervisor/manager/director/VP that needs to LEAD their direct reports to reach their potential instead of just manage them to meet the numbers/KPI's!

If you are interested in learning Get A Klu's Complete Coaching system in either private, group or self-paced/online study, please send an email directly to Jeffrey Klubeck at: jeff@getaklu.net

For now, thank you for reading up on accountability and for any feedback you provide on how the next version of this book can improve OR other topics you would like to see me write about.

All my love ... to YOUR Success!

Jeffrey Klubeck

NOTES

ABOUT THE AUTHOR

At the intersection of academia and business, Jeffrey Klubeck has applied his Master's Degree in Communication to over 20 years of experience in organizational development and transformational business coaching. A coach before it was the trend, Jeffrey has had the opportunity to create performance management and talent recruitment frameworks with organizations such as JP Morgan Chase, State Farm, DOW Pharmaceutical, and King Pharmaceuticals.

With more than 3,000 learners and clients who have actively packed his courses in public speaking, interpersonal, and group communication, Jeff's experience as a former Professor of Communication has created a following of students and coaches who have been able to apply strategic critical thinking and paradigm shifts in their organizations.

Jeffrey has had the pleasure of speaking on 4 continents to audiences from over 40 countries. Jeffrey's teaching, training, and coaching programs have been game changing in helping executives, entrepreneurs, and business teams increase their motivation, accountability, and results!

Discover more at:

www.getaklu.net and www.theklubrary.com

ENJOY A PREVIEW OF
JEFFREY KLUBECK'S UPCOMING BOOK:

THE

INTEGRITY

GAME

To be released in 2021

Da-da-da-da-da-daaa …

"Charge!" the crowd roared in reply to the organ's rally call.

It was the bottom of the ninth inning at Victor Stadium, and the crowd was on its feet, hoping for that one run that would tie the game and send the ball game into extra innings. The sound was deafening as the batter approached the plate, a rookie who had recently been called up from Triple A — now finding himself one of the team's last two shots at scoring a much-needed run.

"Come on, TJ," a middle-aged man said, almost to himself. "You can do it!"

The first pitch crossed the plate, and the umpire's fist signaled strike one. A swing and a miss made the count 0 and 2.

"Slow down, son. Take your time. Make him work for it," the man said.

Almost as if the batter had heard the man's advice, he backed off the next pitch before it crossed the plate and it suddenly took a nosedive into the dirt, before taking a sharp bounce over the catcher's head.

A wild pitch! The crowd was on its feet again as the batter flung his bat and raced toward first base on the dropped third strike...

"Safe!" signaled the first base umpire.

"Atta boy, TJ!" the man exclaimed, this time letting his voice be heard among the crowd.

"Oh great. Leave it to the rookie to make sure we don't get out of here at a decent hour," a sandy-haired vendor moaned to a female coworker from behind the rail. His words were spoken a little louder than intended—just loud enough that they caught the attention of the middle-aged man who stood to their right. Surprised to hear the vendor actually root against the home team, he refused to let it wane his enthusiasm.

"Luke and Tracy, if we go into extra innings, I need you to stick around," said a female voice over the walkie talkie.

"Are you kidding me!" exclaimed the vendor.

"C'mon, Luke, it'll give us a chance to make a few more bucks. Weren't you just complaining about not getting enough tips?" the female spoke.

"But it's Friday night. Tracy, I'm supposed to meet up with the guys after the game. This happens every time I have plans. It's like she's out to get me," Luke complained.

"No, she's not. You heard her—it's our turn. We might as well make the best of it and get ready to restock," Tracy said as she walked toward the concourse.

Muttering something unintelligible under his breath, Luke turned toward the field. Two outs, with a runner on first, and the count was 3 and 1. Just as the pitcher released the ball, the runner on first took off for second. The catcher fired the ball to the second baseman, and to the crowd's disapproval, the batter was called out.

"All right!" Luke yelled.

Again, the man glanced at the vendor, surprised that he was so vocal about hoping that the home team would lose.

"The play is under review," the announcer reported over the loudspeakers.

"Of course it is! Let's just drag this out as long as we can," Luke uttered out loud, refusing to move from the spot where he'd been standing since the beginning of the inning.

Ignoring the vendor's snide comments, the man joined the crowd in watching the replay on the jumbotron. From another angle, the runner was clearly safe and the call was reversed, which sparked the crowd's enthusiasm once again.

"Get a life, people. It's just a game," muttered the vendor.

"Excuse me," the man said. "I couldn't help but overhearing. I take it you're not a Victor fan?"

"Me? I'm a fan, but it's really not that big of a deal. I just wish they'd hurry up and win or hurry up and lose. I've got things to do," Luke replied.

"Hmm, must be really important things you have to do—I mean, to stand among all of your customers and openly root for their team to lose," the man pointed out.

"Hey, you have no clue what you're talking about. Unlike you, I'm here for every game, win or lose. My life revolves around baseball, but baseball isn't everything to everybody," Luke pointed out.

"I might not know what you're talking about," the man admitted. "But I do know a few things. For starters, to some people, baseball is a lot more than *just* a ballgame. It's their dream, their future, their career. It's part of their life, their family, and their traditions. And in case you forgot, it's also a livelihood for the owners, the players, and the staff— even vendors, like you. So, do you mind if I ask why you don't seem to like your job?"

"Maybe I would if things were different," Luke replied.

"Like what things?"

"Like not having to give up Friday night with the guys. Like actually bringing home some decent tips. Like having a boss who would give me a good section once in a while. And having a little fun on the job wouldn't hurt," Luke said, rattling off his responses.

"I guess that is a lot of 'things' not to like. It seems to me that perhaps you didn't come to this job prepared to play."

"What do you mean?"

A roar from the crowd interrupted their conversation, and the men turned toward the field to see a ball fly into deep left field, where to the fans' disappointment, it was caught at the fence.

There were two outs and a runner on second when the manager walked onto the field to make a pitching change.

Turning back to Luke, the man replied, "Let me answer your question with a question. If you don't like your job, what are you doing about it?"

"Nothing. There's nothing I can do. Nobody would listen if I said anything, so why even bother?"

"Oh, I see. So it's better to complain about everything in the world, rather than doing anything about your own world?"

"Hey, that's not fair. You don't even know me ..."

"You're right, I don't. But I've met people like you, and from experience, it isn't just this job you are unhappy with. I'd bet you have something to complain about in ALL the areas of your life ...even the friends you are so eager to hang out with after the game ...I'll bet you complain about from time to time too, right? But they are your friends, and there is nothing you can do about them, right?

"You see, if I am right," the man continued, "then I don't think you can be happy here ... or anywhere, for that matter," the man remarked.

"What are you talking about?" Luke asked.

"I'd be happy to tell you. but first, let me ask you just one more question: Do you believe you have integrity?"

"Sure," Luke answered.

"If you promise not to shoot the messenger, I'll beg to differ, young man. And it's not that you don't have 'any' integrity, but the truth is that we are all out of integrity on some level. That includes me, and that's okay because I believe we never have 100 percent integrity until we die …until we are "re-integrated" with our maker. Until then, we're all human and, yes, we are all flawed…that includes me and it certainly includes you!

"What's integrity got to do with anything?" Luke asked.

"Well, think about things like parenting or driving a car if you don't have kids –there are things we all think WE are good at it while everyone else sucks at it. The same is true with your job. Your boss isn't fair. The fans are cheap. I get it. But I also know that the person who is complaining and accusing others of being out of integrity is usually the person who is actually out of integrity. It's not a judgement, just a fact that it is easier to complain about others than it is to take action and responsibility for ourselves."

"Your name is Luke, right?" the man confirmed.

"Right."

"Nice to meet you, Luke. I'm Terry," the man offered. "For example, I've been standing next to you for some time now. You're complaining about not making enough money, but I haven't seen you try to sell anyone, including me, a hot dog. Why not?"

"Like I said, I'm ready to wrap things up and go home," Luke answered.

The leadoff batter was now at the plate. Almost as if on cue, he shot a groundball just past the shortstop, and the crowd went wild as the rookie, TJ, rounded third and slid into home safely. The game was tied!

"It looks like that's not going to happen," Terry remarked, after he was done applauding.

"Luke, I need you to report *now*," came a firm voice over the walkie talkie.

"Looks like you've got to go, Luke. But I want you to remember that you're not complaining about a baseball game or whether your boss is playing fair. Everything you're complaining about is actually yourself and the fact that you are not winning …heck, perhaps not even playing the game of integrity. In the Integrity Game, you have to be honest with yourself. In the Integrity Game, you have to answer tough questions, make difficult decisions, and take action and responsibility for all of it! If you are tired of a life where you are constantly complaining about other people and 'things' beyond your control…and you believe you're prepared to play, then I think I can help you," the man offered.

"I can't now—didn't you hear, I have to go back to work," Luke replied.

"Oh, I know. But I'll be here until the last pitch is thrown, I assure you. And I'll be back again tomorrow."

"Oh, you have series tickets?"

"No, I'm a season ticket holder. I come to every game to support my son—he's the rookie that started this rally going," Terry smiled proudly. "In our family, baseball is much more than a game … it is a mechanism to learn about life and what separates winners from losers. And in our family, integrity is much more than something we accuse others of not having. Integrity is standard by which the success of all our decisions and actions gets measured! If you take nothing else from our talk, take this: If anything is out of integrity, EVERYTHING is out of integrity!"

"Okay, now you've got my attention. So integrity is really that big of a deal?" Luke asked.

"Not only is it a big deal, young man, I'd say 'it's the ONLY game in town.' I hope I get a chance to teach you how to play … but remember, you have to been honest at all times and ready to look within. You know where to find me tomorrow … and all season long!"

Made in the USA
Monee, IL
16 January 2021